The Machine Learning Toolbox

For Non-Mathematicians

by

D. Brian Letort, PhD

First Edition: January, 2019

Printed in the United States of America

ISBN: 9781794302686

To my wife Brandi, daughter Coraline and
'dogters' Jacey, Belle, and Bailey,
You Mean the World to Me

Table of Contents

Acknowledgement

Many people have contributed to my personal and professional development. First and foremost, my wife Brandi – you fill my life with joy, laughter, and love. Thank you for supporting me in everything we do! Also, I send my appreciation to the many mentors, executives, and peers at Northrop Grumman. In no particular order, Steve Erwin, Rodger McClain, Mark Graham, Bernie McVey, Dawn Meyer, Brad Furukawa, Todd Norwood, Shawn Soeder, Jamie Aksel, Mike Lefler, Richard Vitek, and many others I know I am forgetting. You all challenged me, motivated me, and supported me in bettering our business while supporting my professional development.

Preface

A revolution has occurred within computer networking and the internet that has enabled new platforms and communication techniques. Without these advancements, the leisure provided by the social media giants of Facebook, Twitter, Instagram, and others would not be possible. Likewise, instant access to our friends and families via a mobile phone call or text message would not be possible. Finally, access to our favorite websites are only a few swipes or keystrokes away. Just as these advancements have altered our behavior, machine learning has begun to follow a similar route, and many of us do not realize its presence. For instance, the more we shop at Amazon, the better the recommendations become. Facebook makes it simple to identify faces for tagging individuals. The United States Postal Service uses handwritten recognition to route mail. And the examples could continue across all areas of our business and professional lives. This book is founded on the principle that in the future, everyone in an Information Technology-type role will need awareness of Machine Learning. Additionally, this book will arm our readers with a common toolbox of machine learning algorithms. What makes this book different is my attempt to reduce the complications of the inherent mathematics and statistics. While both are critical to the use of the discussed algorithms, I believe there is an alternate approach that can explain the algorithms without their complexity. So, this book will be useful to IT management from a high-level vantage and targeted to software engineers, systems engineers, and other IT-related roles to establish the foundational knowledge and application of Machine Learning algorithms. I hope you find this book as useful and fun as it was for me to assemble.

Historical Perspective

COMPUTER PROGRAMMING

Computer programming dates back to Charles Babbage and his construction of a difference engine. The goal of his invention was to apply machinery to assist with calculations and computations across nautical navigation and the astronomical and mathematical underpinnings. So theoretically, we could say this device overcame some of the redundant and mundane tasks that existed prior to this invention.

Some of the major milestones that enabled software programming to emerge included time-shared Mainframe computers of the 1960s, structured programming (e.g., Cobal, Pascal, C, etc.) in the 1960s, Microcomputers of the 1970s (e.g., Commodore, Tandy, Apple, IBM, etc.), and the birth and growth of the internet in the 1980s. During these advancements, software programming fell into an identity crisis. During a 1968 NATO conference, a theory was proposed that software should follow established engineering practices (Randell, 1968). Following this proposal, computer programming began to formalize under systematic approaches. Shortly after this, Winston Royce proposed the waterfall method as a process for engineering software, which is still widely used today. Given software is intangible compared to other engineering disciplines, this adoption took time to be accepted. Without these foundational advancements, it could be argued that the computer architectures and software deployment environments of machine learning algorithms would be amiss. This is due to the simple fact that computer systems create the very data that allows machine learning algorithms to flourish. Additionally, many hardware advancements occurred between these times that enabled parallel processing, distributed computing, and streaming data feeds. These developments enabled the "Big Data" aspects of Machine Learning.

If we fast forward to modern day computers, computers still exist to achieve the same original goal of Babbage, albeit with much more complicated devices. Even modern-day vehicles average 100M lines of software code. Said another way, when evaluating a new vehicle to purchase, it is highly likely that software technology is a large factor. Consider the following list that details how much software exists in modern systems and products (Desjardins, 2017).

- The control software to run a U.S. military drone uses 3.5 million lines of code.
- A Boeing 787 has 6.5 million lines behind its avionics and online support systems.
- Google Chrome (browser) runs on 6.7 million lines of code (upper estimate).
- A Chevy Volt uses 10 million lines.
- The Android operating system runs on 12-15 million lines.
- The Large Hadron Collider uses 50 million lines.
- Not including backend code, Facebook runs on 62 million lines of code.
- With the advent of sophisticated, cloud-connected infotainment systems, the car

software in a modern vehicle apparently uses 100 million lines of code.
- All Google services combine for a whopping 2 billion lines.

A million lines of code, if printed, would be about 18,000 pages of text. Therefore, applying the math above –it would take 36,000,000 pages to "print out" all of the code behind all Google services. That would be a stack of paper 2.2 miles high!

Just as Babbage invented a device to assist with calculations, this could be described as static calculations. In a modern sense, we would call this an algorithm. For instance, let us assume we are coding a payroll application. In this activity, we need data and the rules to apply to such data. The data would likely include hours worked and labor rates. The rules would be when to apply base time, time-and-a-half, double time, etc. Therefore, these are the static rules are our algorithm.

Consider the following diagram that conceptualizes traditional computer programming / software engineering:

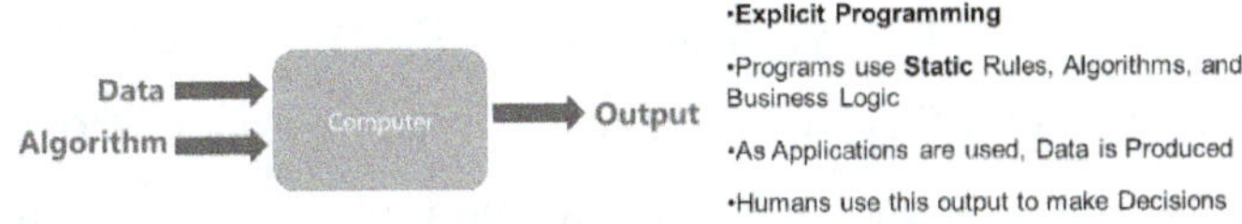

We can see the rules can be applied in the algorithm, data is required as parameters to the algorithm, and the output would result from the static rules. This is the fundamental principle of most computer programs.

MACHINE LEARNING

Machine Learning differs vastly from traditional programming and software engineering. The primary difference is that static rules are uncovered within the patters of data versus, defining the rules up-front. Said another way, machine learning algorithms, often called "algos" for short, are used to identify such patterns. In this context, we could define learning as, recognizing complex patterns in historical data, under the assumption that history will repeat itself and these patterns will hold true in the upcoming future.

To accomplish the learning aspect of machine learning, many approaches are included, such as probability theory, traditional statistics, control theory, search, and combinational optimization. These approaches can be applied to various data elements, such as textual, visual, robotics, game theory, and many other areas. This leads to application of language translation, financial forecasting, weather forecasting, games, robotics, self-driven cars, and many areas in-between.

Some of the key milestones that enabled machine learning include:

- The Turing Test in 1950, which attempts to determine if real intelligence exists by fooling a human to believe the computer is human.

- In 1957, the first neural network using a perceptron was constructed.

- In 1967, the nearest neighbor (e.g., kNN) was written for basic pattern recognition.

- In 1979, students at Stanford developed the Stanford Cart that navigated obstacles in a room.

-   In 1997, IBM's Deep Blue beats the world champion in chess.

-   In 1985, Terry Sejnowski and Charles Rosenberg utilized an artificial neural network to teach itself how to correctly pronounce 20K words in a week.

-   In 2006, Geoffrey Hinton coins the term "deep learning" for a new set of algorithms that advance traditional Machine Learning for use with images and video.

-   In 2011 IBM's Watson beats human competitors in Jeopardy.

-   In 2011, Google Brain is developed to identify visual objects.

-   In 2014, Facebook develops DeepFace, which is an algorithm that is able to recognize individuals and faces.

-   In 2014, the Chatbot "Eugene Goostman" passes the Turing test and convinced 33% of its judges that it was an Ukrainian teen.

- In 2016, the Googles AI platform beats a professional player at the Chinese board game "Go", which is said to be one of the world's most complex board games.

This progression established Machine Learning as the basis for many innovative companies. Some common examples are: use to separate email spam, Amazon product recommendations, Facebook facial recognition for tagging, Uber route optimization, self-driving cars, and many other examples. What separates Machine Learning from traditional programming is that the computer identifies trends and patterns, which dynamically defines the algorithm. Consider the figure below, which illustrates this point:

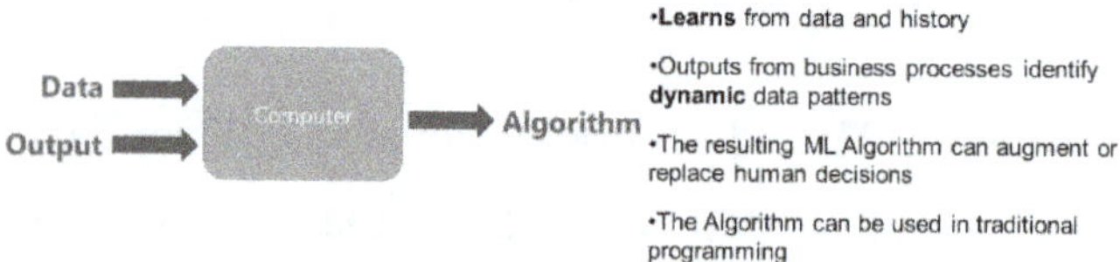

Machine Learning is rooted in statistical and programming methods. This occurs via making the assumption that history will repeat itself. So, if this concept holds true, an algorithm can be derived that is applied to future scenarios. This, in turn, allows us to make predictions and optimize our choices to prescribe to the optimal outcome.

Three major advancements have enabled the widespread use of machine learning, which include the massive growth of data, expansion of data management tools, and more powerful computer processing options.

The massive growth of data, often called 'Big Data' is described as the Variety, Volume, and Velocity of new data sources. From a variety vantage, no longer is structured data the only valuable sources for algorithms to utilize. Now, images, audio, streaming sensory information, and many other sources can be utilized. Traditionally, Relational Database Management Systems (RDMBS) were the primary data storage technique. These are based on relational algebra and the use of Structured Query Language (SQL). RDBMS primarily thrived with structured data in sizes up to around a few hundred Terabytes. While this could be increased, the architecture and hardware required becomes quite expensive. This variety requires us to utilize new data storage technologies, such as Hadoop and other NoSQL (Not Only SQL) technologies. Hadoop, the most widely known, is based on distributed programming and the concept that we can shard data (e.g., spread it across) hundreds or thousands of servers. When data is spread in such a way, when our data is queried, it runs on every server, providing massive parallelism. So, Hadoop brings the processing to the data, rather than the data to the processing, as in relational database engines. For this reason, Hadoop has emerged as the leading technology to assist with the Volume and Velocity aspects, in addition to Variety.

The expansion of data management tools spans many areas. While Hadoop has emerged as a large ecosystem of sub-tools, other NoSQL technologies also exist. Just as RDBMS is based on relational queries, NoSQL databases are based on other storage techniques, such as Key-Values, Columnar, Graph, or Document database types. The emergence and vast growth of these database technologies has been driven by the various variety types of data.

Finally, more powerful processing options arises from the use of parallel processing systems in Hadoop and NoSQL systems as well as through the use of Graphical Processing Units (GPUs). GPUs are far superior to Central Processing Units (CPUs) within modern computers via having the ability to offload work from CPUs into a high-bandwidth optimized instruction pipeline.

The expansion of these areas has perpetuated vast opportunities for not only machine learning, but for the base platform of many critical internet companies. See the figure below by Lori Lewis (2018).

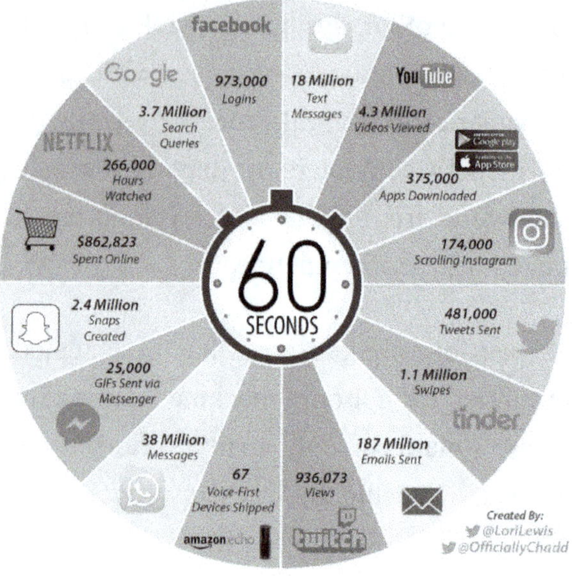

As noted by Lewis, in 2018, enormous activity occurs each minute. Comparing this to prior years, the expansion is expected to continue to increase year-over-year. These platforms are heavily rooted to these newer data management tools and machine learning techniques. As more people expand their use across these digital experiences, we can expect an expansion of machine learning as well. This will improve our experience via automating mundane tasks, optimizing our schedules, saving money, and making recommendations to improve our qualities of live.

Definitions

As with any emerging technology, buzzwords and jargon is often present. Due to this, conflicting ideals, theories, and terminology arises. Essentially, the nebulousness should be deconflicted via establishing common definitions. To accomplish this, the following section will do so across the fields of general artificial intelligence, data science, machine learning, and deep learning. Consider the following image as the foundation for these definitions:

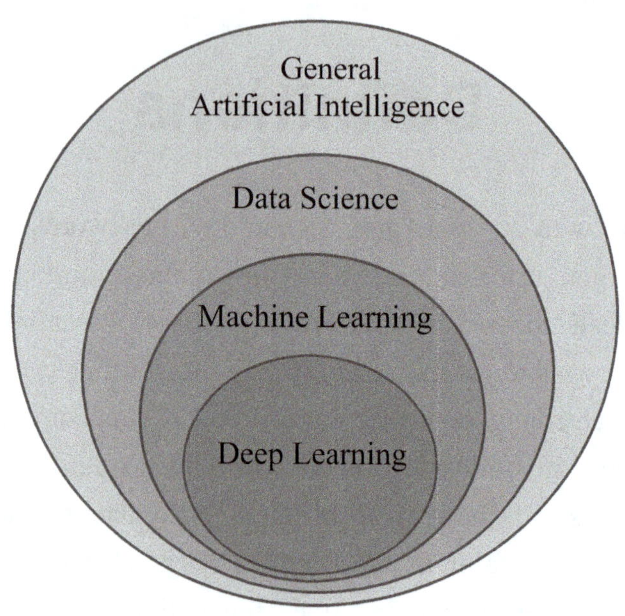

GENERAL ARTIFICIAL INTELLIGENCE

In 1956 the Dartmouth Summer Research Project on Artificial Intelligence occurred. This occurance included 11 scientists and mathematicians as the seminal event that would establish the foundational research for Artificial Intelligence. The original proposal for this event can be found at http://raysolomonoff.com/dartmouth/boxa/dart564p rops.pdf. To quote the key key scope:

> "We propose that a 2 month, 10 man study of artificial intelligence be carried out during the summer of 1956 at Dartmouth College in Hanover, New Hampshire. The study is to proceed on the basis of the conjecture that every aspect of learning or any other feature of intelligence can in principle be so precisely described that a machine can be made to simulate it. An attempt will be made to find how to make machines use language, form abstractions and concepts, solve kinds of problems now reserved for humans, and improve themselves. We think that a significant advance can be made in one or more of these problems if a carefully selected group of scientists work on it together for a summer." (McCarthy et al., 1955)

This event established the original definition, success criteria, and underlying goals of developing Artificial Intelligence. This development had influence across many areas of academia, professional organizations, and even Hollywood. The proposed use of Artificial Intelligence aim to achieve equality with the human brain. To accomplish this, advancements would be required to provide many functions, such as:

- Problem Solving
- Judgement
- Anticipation
- Speaking an expressive language
- Reading/Writing
- Visual Perception
- Spatial Perception
- Personality
- Memory retention/recall
- Learning
- Ability to take Action
- Feelings

Accomplishing these functions is a large feat. The ability to accomplish even a portion of this largely led to the first 'Artificial Intelligence Winter' in the 1970s-1980s. This 'Winter' was a time where the promises of the technological advancement did not meet expectations and the overly hyped benefit. However, during this time, some other seminal advancements were achieved in related areas that led to the birth of Data Science, Machine Learning, and eventually Deep Learning. While the term Data Science has been around in research since the 1950s, it wasn't until 2008 that DJ Patil and Jeff Hammerbacker, then at Facebook and LinkedIn, started using the term Data Scientist for its current context. This new context involves using new technologies, such as Hadoop and NoSQL (e.g., Not Only SQL), as well as newer Machine Learning Approaches that were maturing, exponentially. While some algorithms existed in the 1950s, such as k-Nearest Neighbor, the more popular foundational algorithms were uncovered in the 1980s thru early 2000s. Some of these include Decision Trees, Support Vector Machines, randomforest, and Adaptive Boosting. These, and others, will be covered later in the book. Deep Learning, on the other hand, has been in and out of the limelight since the 1950s and again is at the forefront in the 2010s. This is largely due to the simple fact that deep learning algorithms flourish with large datasets and with the dramatic growth from the prior decade, algorithms established much earlier are now performing better. Therefore, we can conclude that Big Data required new approaches, such as Deep

Learning, to realize patterns in such complex datasets.

DATA SCIENCE

It has been said that the Data Scientist is the 'Sexiest Job of the 21st Century'. The Data Science role was brought into the spotlight via many popular successes. Examples include IBM Watson winning on Jeopardy, Target being able to predict teen pregnancy, the notorious Kaggle Netflix challenge, and widespread use across retail and social media providers to improve brand awareness, sales, and other benefits. Given the data scientist must have a mix of programming, math/statistics, and business knowledge, it is often said that data scientists are 'Unicorns', meaning they do not exist. The figure below illustrates the intersection of these three skills.

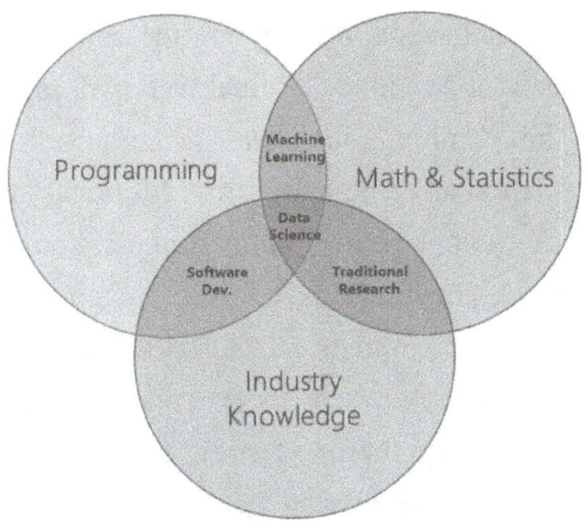

Programming involves using languages such as R, Python, Java, C/C++ as well as commercial software packages such as SAS, SPSS, Matlab, and many others. Math and statistics are the foundational aspects of extracting patterns within the identified and hypothesized datasets. The amount of Math and Statistics knowledge required depends on the specific goals for a project. For example, if just using existing R or Python libraries, just knowing 'pseudocode' level will suffice. If attempting to construct an algorithm from scratch or implementing on an embedded system, knowledge of the underlying math and stats is required. However, some very basic understandings are required. This includes understanding the common data types such as Nominal, Ordinal, Interval, and Ratio and the common statistical techniques to identify correlation as well as causation is critical to the success of a data scientist. For example, some algorithms need encoding to convert categorical columns to numeric columns. Other skills in this realm may include research theory and design, survey design, hypothesis testing, parameter estimation, and other from statistical theory. From an industry knowledge, having an understanding of the business process area is critical to the successful application. For instance, let's assume we are trying to forecast headcounts within a Work Breakdown Structure (WBS) of an organization. Let's assume we have the WBS of 3002210531. How do we know what this number really means? Perhaps the first three is the Cost Center, the next Four are the Account, and the final three are the Contract. Taking this a step further, how do we know if the Cost Center is General and Administrative (e.g., Overhead) or Direct Charge? All these questions come into play when we try to extract patterns from our data.

One trend that has emerged is that simple skills often go a very long way and not every project requires advanced programming. Consider this KDNuggets survey of tools from 2015-2017:

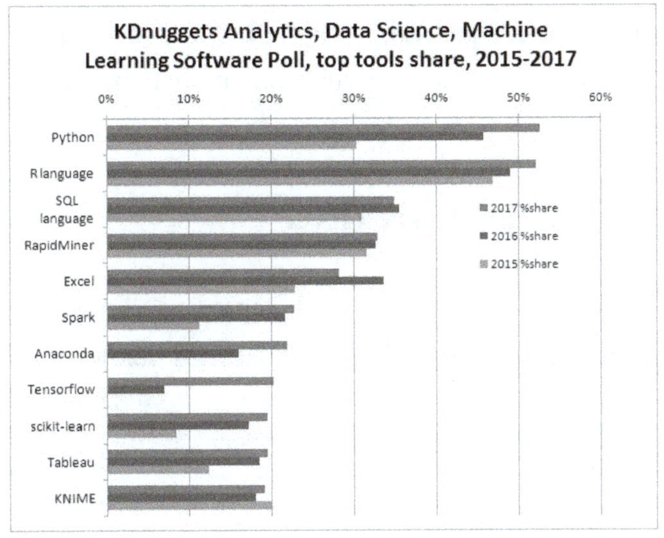

Figure 1 - 2017 Data Science Tools (Piatetsky, 2018)

Elaborating on this diagram, we see a continued growth of both Python and R as well as a good portion of SQL and Excel still in existence, although both are on the decline.

To complicate these complex skills, data engineering, which includes the skills to build data ingest pipelines, transform, move large amounts of data, and define how the data is stored, is also a skill data scientist should be aware of, if not able to perform. However, the primary skills desired by the data scientist are based on the ability to apply statistical analysis and machine learning techniques. This will be the basis of subsequent chapters of this book.

MACHINE LEARNING

Machine Learning can be separated into five different categories, which is illustrated below:

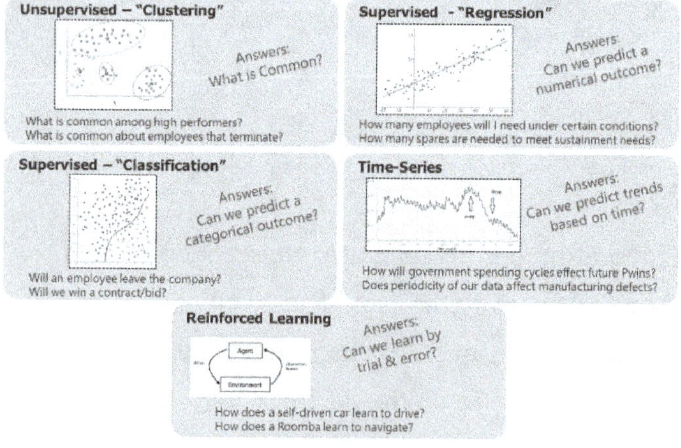

Unsupervised Machine Learning involves techniques, which do not try to predict an outcome. Rather they either try to identify what is common or try to provide recommendations. Consider product recommendations. By segmenting by age alone, we are able to derive potential recommendations. For instance, less than 10 years old would likely infer recommendations for toys. Ages 10-20 may make recommendations about the latest electronic gadgets or common sports products as toddler toys would likely not resonate. When we combine additional data, such as gender or even preferences, we can likely derive additional recommendations.

Supervised learning involves predicting either a numerical or categorical outcome. In supervised learning, our goal is to identify independent variable(s) (IVs) that are related to and predict dependent variable(s) (DVs). This is often illustrated as a causal diagram. The ultimate goal of supervised learning is to use historical information to create a model that predicts and generalizes on future, unseen data. This assumes that history will repeat itself. One key principle of supervised learning involves the theory of the curse of dimensionality, which states that the larger the IV feature space, the more difficult it is to create an accurate algorithm. So generally speaking, supervised algorithms perform best with a smaller set of IVs towards predicting the DV. We will cover the various algorithms that span predicting numerical and categorical outcomes in later chapters.

Reinforced learning is similar to supervised learning, however, rather than a data scientist training, testing, validating, and deploying an algorithm, an agent is created. This agent contains a reward system that provides feedback on if the decision was correct or not. After hundreds, thousands, or even millions of observations, the feedback eventually trains the algorithm to perform well in an autonomous manner.

DEEP LEARNING

Deep Learning is a relatively new field within Machine Learning that is based on Deep Neural Networks. Being 'Deep', many hidden layers exist between the input and output layers. The following image illustrates a simple neural network architecture compared to a deep learning network architecture (Edwards, 2018). Note the many layers as hidden.

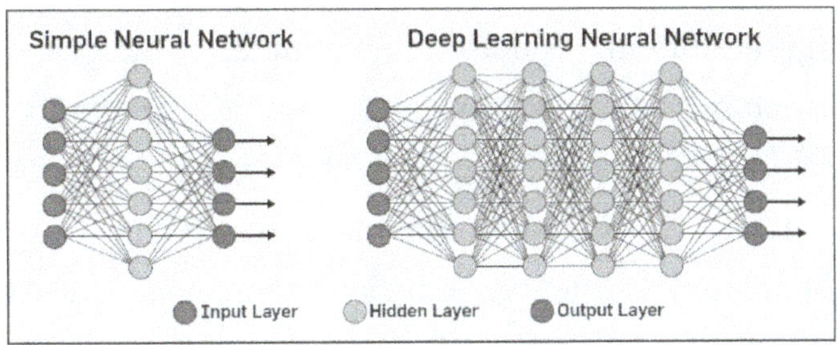

Deep Learning is especially useful for complex problems and large datasets. Common uses include automatic speech recognition, speech translation (across languages), image recognition, image restoration, natural language generation, drug toxicology, and many other scenarios. For automatic speech recognition, we often encounter this when calling helpdesks or support lines. These systems prompt users to speak the choice and route appropriately. Speech translation is widely used to convert from languages, such as English to Spanish. Image Recognition has many applications, such as classifying an image or finding a particular object within an image. Given video is essentially many image frames combined, video analysis or automated decisions based on sensory is possible, such as with an unmanned automobile or aircraft. Image restoration assists with enhancing old photos, partial photos, or even removing objects within a high-definition photo. Natural Language Generation is especially useful for title generation from a news article, or even with bots that allow for someone to ask questions and respond. Drug Toxicology is often very difficult to manage, due to the many variables – however, deep neural networks thrive with such large datasets.

Machine Learning Roles

In today's rapidly evolving and competitive landscape, organizations are pressured to find new ways to leverage innovation for competitive advantage. Given the massive amount of data being created and used in various capacities, new roles have emerged. These roles span many areas including data preparation, data storage, applying algorithms, visualizing, and applying to business processes. Some of the common roles that exist include data scientist, citizen data scientist, data engineer, data steward, business analyst, and visualization expert.

DATA SCIENTIST

Data Scientists are often referred to as Unicorns due to the large marketing and hype surrounding the application of data science to complex organizational datasets. This role emerged from the prior roles of statisticians and software engineering. As mentioned previously, to apply within a business context, the data scientist should be skilled in three areas – Math/Statistics, Computer Programming, and Business Processes where the data science is being applied.

The level needed within Math and Statistics will vary depending on the complexity of the problem, technology, and language being used. For instance, in a typical business setting, the data scientist may be using R or Python and with common libraries, such as the popular R caret or Python Scikit-learn packages. These packages enable the 'black box' application of the algorithms. While the data scientists doesn't necessarily need to understand the detailed implementation of these packages, they should understand how they work at a high-level or pseudocode-level. Newer tools, which are based on drag-and-drop canvases, such as Rapidminer, may reduce the mathematics and remove the programming requirement all together. However, if applying an algorithm within an embedded system, such as on an automobile or aircraft, then lower level languages, such as C are needed along with a deep understanding of the mathematics and statistics of the algorithmic approach. Meaning, caret or Scikit-learn are not available on embedded Operating Systems.

Similar to the level of detail needed for Math and Statistics, the amount of programming skills required often depends on the specific application. Python and R are often the leading tools of choice by a data science, due to the large amount of libraries available. Contributors have created libraries that allow for a data scientist to leverage by passing data through. Recent trends even include using algorithms as a service from suppliers such as

Algorithmia as well as automatic Machine Learning from suppliers such as DataRobot.

No matter the tool or situation, having the detailed context for the business setting is required for any data scientist to succeed. For example, assume we are writing algorithms for a factor floor that produces some manufactured product and our goal is to predict defects as this project is assembled. Defects would be captured in some way with some notation for the type of defect (e.g., out of tolerance, missing part, defective part, etc.). Knowing how the assembly process works, supplier parts process, and quality assurance process may all be required to have an understanding of what input columns have predictive power.

CITIZEN DATA SCIENTIST

When Information Technology (IT) departments first emerged, they did so under the authoritarian-type approach that all aspects of IT should be governed and provided from this department. This would include networking, server support, software engineering, database administration, information security, and many other fields. This was due to the simple fact that most business employees had little to no IT knowledge. And employees in the IT department had degrees in computer science-oriented fields as well as certifications and other forms of training. Additionally, during the early days of the authoritarian IT departments, employees likely had more technology at work than at home. Therefore, unless an employee worked in the IT field, they likely knew little about technology. However, if we fast-forward to modern times, employees likely have more technology at home than at work. Some even call the younger or 'Millennial Generation' digital natives. This group is the largest by far entering our workforce with roughly 10 thousand entering the workforce every other day. By the year 2025, it is estimated that the millennial age generation will comprise 75% of the workforce. The Millennial age generation did not experience the use of dial-up internet versus high-speed internet, dictionaries instead of Google, Blockbuster instead of Netflix, and film development instead of digital photography. These technologies have shaped expectations in the workforce as well as promoting an environment where this workforce is highly skilled in many IT fields. Being a digital native is not always bounded to age alone. Generation X or Baby Boomers who have followed the shifts in technology to modern times can hold the same expectations, behavioral patterns, and knowledge of IT roles, but reside outside of the IT department.

This leads to a situation where the business user may be fairly diverse with their knowledge of the typical IT roles. Therefore, it has become acceptable and common to allow for 'Citizen' type of IT work from a non-IT role. These citizen roles often have typical business titles, such as 'Accountant', 'Supply Chain Analyst', 'Systems Engineer', or many others. And, they would use lightweight IT tools to create IT-like products. This could be smaller software 'Apps', Visualization Reports, or even relatively simple algorithms. Data Science has followed this trend. While most data scientist use R or Python, the citizen roles would likely use drag-and-drop tools, such as IBM SPSS, RapidMiner, or Orange Canvas. At this time, citizen roles are often discussed in many areas such as Citizen Software Developer, Citizen Data

Steward, and others, but within the analytics arena, citizen data science is the most popular.

DATA ENGINEER

The simple definition of a data engineer is someone who provides the right data to the right person at the right time. Traditionally, this involves using Extract, Transform, and Load (ETL) or Extract, Load, and Transform (ELT) tools. ETL tools, such as SQL Server Integration Services (SSIS), Alteryx, or Informatica are commonly used. These tools create workflows that connect to data sources via flat files, database connections, web services, or other end-poitns to acquire data, then perform any cleaning, filtering, joining, or other preparation and structuring required before placing the data in the final location. This final location is often a database, but could be flat files, XML, or other commonly used data types. ELT tools are often based on Big Data Technologies, such as Hadoop. In an ELT scenario, the data is stored first, then transformed for subsequent use. For instance, a dataset may be stored on Hadoop Distributed File System (HDFS) and then exposed through a HIVE query that is added to the data after it is stored. This HIVE example of ELT is referred to as 'Schema on Read', whereas ETL is referred to as 'Schema on Write'. Circling back to ETL, which involves relational databases, the data engineer must know how the data is to be used prior to storage. And this use may lead to the storage of the same data multiple times. For example, we may normalize to 3rd normal form for efficiency, have a flattened copy of a table for tabular reporting, and have a copy placed in a star schema for Ad Hoc analysis via Online Analytical Processing (OLAP) cubes. In all ETL scenarios, the database schema must be created before the data is loaded. Compared to ELT, this is not the case. ELT is common for exploratory work when we are not sure how we want to query the data.

Data engineering is important to the data scientist as the techniques specialize in the proper management and exposure of data for subsequent use. For instance, a Data Scientist may attempt to use R or Python for data engineering. Under this scenario, unless many SQL or other native languages are used within R or Python, the data is stored in memory on the computer being used. Therefore, severe limitations likely exist. Rather, if ETL and ETL tools are used, they place the data in a database and keep the data in the database for any altering. Then expose it for connectivity with R or Python.

The new role of a Citizen Data Engineer has emerged that is similar to the citizen data scientist. This has occurred due to a new set of tools emerging, which are called Self-Service Data Prep tools. An example is Alteryx. These tools follow drag-and-drop approaches that allows a non-data engineering to conduct the common ETL and ELT tasks. For instance, if connecting to a database, a visual screen generates the SQL language needed, rather than constructing from scratch. One could argue that Excel is a citizen data engineering too. While this does hold some truth, excel is often limited by the amount of data stored. Newer add-ins, such as the PowerQuery add-in, does improve the user experience, but the data is typically stored in excel, which introduces the limits, when compared to a database.

DATA STEWARD

Within the data science and analytics community, a common term that is often stated is that "Garbage In, Garbage Out". This alludes to the need for quality data for any analytics activity. To mitigate this problem, the role of an information or data steward emerged. These roles are often assigned to particular business functions and work with the business data owners to ensure proper controls, governance, and processes are in place to uphold the integrity of data quality. Often these roles work closely with any data cataloging effort to register datasets so they can be searched and used with the proper security controls.

BUSINESS ANALYST

The business analyst is a common role that augments all aspects of analytics. They may have various titles, but the commonality exists in that they know the business process area very well. When a data scientist has questions regarding the digital trail left in data, the business analyst is leveraged to explain. If problematic business processes are identified, the business analyst would lead the effort to correct. The business analyst can also assist with data engineering activities. If a data engineer needs to understand how datasets can be combined, the business analyst assists with explaining the process of data creation and characteristics of transactions effecting any changes.

VISUALIZATION EXPERT

The visualization expert in an analytics activity may be a separate role, or could be fulfilled by a data scientist. With either approach, the primary objective is to represent the analytics activity and findings in a way that resonates with the intended audience. Often, the use of story-telling is leveraged as a mechanism to create a narrative and dialog that further engage the audience. Some of the activities needed in this role is to assess the types of data across numerical, categorical, time-series and determine the best way to visualization with barcharts, piecharts, heatmaps, and many others. Also, the proper use of color is considered. When these aspects are synthesized, the analytics artifacts can be assembled, presented, and used to communicate the findings that assist in achieving the intended goals. These goals could be influencing adoption, raising awareness, guiding cultural change, or producing a prediction for subsequent use.

The Machine Learning Process

CRISP-DM

Many efforts have occurred in academic and professional settings that aim to establish robust and repeatable process, which in turn aims to achieve a predictable product. In areas such as Software Engineering, the likes of CMMI, IDEAL, ISO, Six Sigma, and many others have emerged and been adopted for this reason. Similarly, in the world of data science, repeatable process models have also emerged. While a few years old now, an interesting survey reveals the CRoss Industry Standard Process for Data Mining (CRISP-DM), Sample, Explore, Modify, Model, and Assess (SEMMA), Knowledge Discovery in Databases (KDD), and organic process models are commonly used (Piatetsky, 2014). Similarly, in a study by Piatetsky, Azevedo, and Santos (2008), it was found that CRISP-DM is both the most popular and most complete lifecycle, when compared to SEMMA and KDD. Building upon this, the CRISP-DM process is now being merged with agile software development methodologies in the form of 'AnalyticsOps' (Grady et al., 2017). Drawing similarities to DevOps, these benefits are realized when combined with flexible and automated infrastructure and deeply integrated Application Lifecycle Management (ALM) and deployment processes. The value of AnalyticsOps is realized when automation occurs via the promotion of an algorithm to the production environment. Many predict that in the near future, software development projects will utilize a Machine Learning role. When this occurs, we can expect AnalyticsOps to unify with DevOps. This increased automation will still utilize CRISP-DM, but optimize the manual steps, such as code promotion, versioning, infrastructure management, etc, when possible.

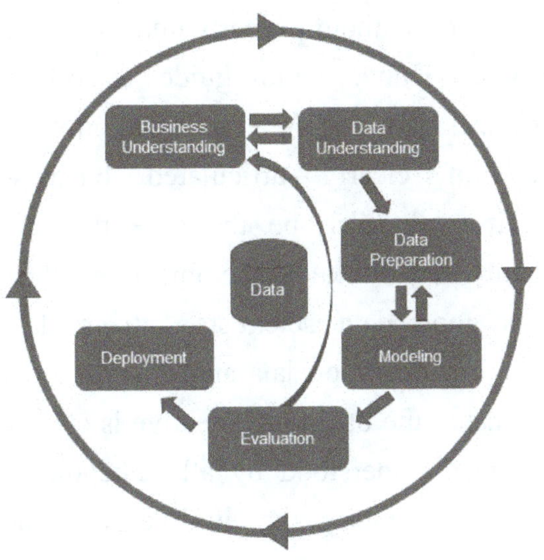

Just as any repeatable process, the risk for being unsuccessful lies in the omission to follow the intended steps. Experience illustrates that four common problems occur during the execution of the CRISP-DM process (Taylor, 2017). These include a lack of business understanding clarity, mindless rework, blind handoff from the data scientist to the Information Technology Department, and failure to iterate.

When introduced to a new business problem, it is often difficult to separate the symptoms from problems. Additionally, it is also tempting to jump strait into a solution without properly understanding the requirements. Human nature guides us to help when issues arise, so it is often tempting to omit the critical step of clearly articulated business objectives. It could also be the case that the requesting entity may not know the objective either. Therefore, as good data scientists, citizen data scientists, data engineers, or data analysts, our goal should be to ensure the business objective is clearly captured and well understood by all stakeholders and contributors. Doing so will ensure the following steps are built upon a solid foundation.

As data scientists, we are eager and motivated to use our favorite language or tool to ingest data, sit on the edge of our seats, and eagerly uncover the wonderful story the data reveals. In CRISP-DM, this occurs across the four steps of Data Understanding, Data Preparation, Modeling, and Evaluation. During our first iteration of these steps, the reality is we often miss opportunities to reveal better insights for many reasons, such as missing details in data, assumptions with our preparation, decisions on modeling techniques, and many other reasons. All this could culminate into mindless rework, which is essentially not being able to meet the business objectives or aimlessly producing results with no success criteria identified. This could be a direct result of poor data quality, improper data preparation, time constraints, inaccessibility to the correct data, or limited knowledge of the needed modeling techniques. Additionally, it often takes enormous time to squeeze out a bit of better performance of our modeling technique and we must ask if it is really worth the effort. Therefore, mindless rework is related to a lack of clarity as well as the expectation that the outcomes may take a slight turn from the original goals.

The blind handoff to IT makes the assumption the duties are separated from the team performing the analytics versus the team supporting the analytics. Deployment of an algorithm could take many different paths, such as publishing as a web service, publishing as a stored procedure in a database, as app like R Shiny or those similar, in notebooks such as Jupyter and others, or even with the local language such as C# or Java on the infrastructure supporting the app, as well as many other scenarios.

This opportunity likely emerges when an algorithm or other form of analytic is embedded within an application. For instance, consider a recommendation system on a website supported by a software engineering group in IT. In this scenario, the software engineer may just make a REST call to the web service and likely has limited knowledge of the innerworkings of the algo, but must know how to interact with it. In this situation, the software engineer needs to know how to pass data to the REST endpoint and what to expect in return after the data is processed. Likewise, the model builder must understand the data that is to be passed. So, we can conclude that collaboration on both sides are required for deployment, use, and sustainment.

One thing that is common with analytical algorithms and the production solutions is that they are not without support and maintenance. For instance, if we train an algorithm on historical data, it makes the assumption those patters persist into the future. However, in today's competitive and agile environment, business processes and its associated data does evolve. When a business process changes, it is likely the data changes. This, in turn, may turn a good algorithm into being useless. Therefore, algorithms will need to evolve as well. Ensuring the model performance is continually evaluated is needed to avoid the model becoming outdated.

COMMON STEPS

BUSINESS UNDERSTANDING

All project lifecycle processes have many things in common. One of those is the simple fact that before any work must be done, we must understand the scope and boundaries of the project. This is true for traditional engineering processes and data science processes alike. Therefore, when a data science project begins or is being evaluated for feasibility to begin, the data scientist and the associated team members must understand, in business terms, what the customer wants to accomplish. Additionally, how the desired outcome and deliverable will be utilized should also be discussed. For instance, if a predictive model is requested to meet a clearly articulated business objective, the customer and stakeholder should discuss its use and how it enables value. More importantly, the definition of value should be agreed upon as well. In this context, value often comes in improved speed, reduced risk, improved quality, or reduced cost.

The first step is to assess the current situation. Most business processes are captured in command media. Some of these are audited (e.g., SOX, HIPAA etc.), so likely more accurate than others. In any case, the documented processes are always a good starting point when evaluating an area that is interested in data science. Upon evaluating the as-is state and current situation, an understand of the business process and associated resources should be captured. Some projects may additionally capture functional and non-functional requirements of the to-be state and solution. These should include success criteria to ensure requirements satisfaction has been met. For larger and more critical projects, they may even include a full project lifecycle, such as the creation of artifacts across: system scope, requirements, architecture, design, coding, testing, and even maintenance.

The next step is to understand how the business processes are reflected in the available data. As data scientists and analysts, our activities include using the available data to achieve stakeholder goals. The importance of the business understanding and as-is state becomes important as we gain access to the data, under the assumption that the data reflects the business process. Many times, identifying where the data resides as well as how to gain access is a large effort in itself. Once this occurs, we can begin to focus on the data understanding.

DATA UNDERSTANDING

The data understanding phase is when the particular data is identified and acquired. This is often the longest aspect of the data science lifecycle due to red tape and access restrictions that are often in place. The data scientist will likely work with a data engineer to extract, filter, combine, cleanse, and any other data engineering activities to proper prepare the data. If the dataset is small and relatively clean, then the data science tools may suffice. However, this is often the exception, rather than the rule. Therefore, data engineers have a key role in the data understanding phase.

Once the data is acquired, the data scientist will likely work to understand what each column or 'feature' represents. Many call this the sub-task under Data Understanding as the 'Analyze Data' activities. Considerations, such as the data type of Nominal, Ordinal, Interval, and Ratio occur, which lead to how each column may or may not be used. Additionally, the actual meaning of fields need to be understood. For instance, if we are evaluating a Cost Center feature, it may be useful to know that anything in the 300s is material and anything in the 600s is Overhead. Meaning, if we are trying to find patterns to predict material defects, we may only filter on the 3xx cost centers. Given the business process 'exhaust' creates the data to be left behind, a business analyst is often included to assist with this deep understanding

Let's consider the below fictional budgeting and earned value data:

Rec Type	Fin Plan	WBS	Acct	CC	OP	EOC	Cat	Period	Total Hours	Regular Hours
E	071A	A4044099011123453452	8851	310	0	M	40	201807	4483	5991
A	181A	C4135439012556774796	7765	813	0	O	25	201812	4172	2121
B	191B	C4349878011999112498	3342	220	0	Y	25	201907	2752	5336
D	192B	A4004299011003992498	1123	311	0	O	26	202012	8352	6667

Understanding the business process could lead to many questions, such as:

- How is this data used? Is it for budget adjustments for underrun/overrun reallocation? How are engineering change orders and other contract modifications reflected?

- What does the record type mean? 'A' could mean Annual Operation Plan, 'E' could mean Estimate at Completion, 'D' could be a Divisional Operating Budget, etc. Each of these have implications for their use towards budgeting and forecasting.

- What constitutes the Work Breakdown Structure (WBS)? Perhaps it could be decomposed as the following:

  - Position 1 = work package prefix

- o   Position 2-4 = contract identifier

- o   Positions 5-11 = work package suffix

- o   Position 12-16 = general ledger number

- o   Position 17-20 = Tail number

- Perhaps CC's in the 300s could be Material related, 6-700s could be G&A related, and 200s could be direct costs to a particular contract.

- How would one separate EOC or "Element of Cost" as Material, Time, etc.?

- What does category mean and how is it used by the business?

- For the Period, does it represent a cumulative or instance in time?

- What are the rules to define the various Actual Cost of Work Performed (ACWP), Budgeted Cost of Work Scheduled (BCWS), and Budgeted Cost of Work Performed (BCWP) fields for earned value purposes?

- Missing columns could also be a concern. For instance, if this is at a detailed level, the work station for the actual manufacturing may be required. Knowing to look for and inquire about this would be important.

Having a business understanding allows us to dive into these details and properly prepare data. This can also help with additional aspects, such as missing values, outliers, skewness, and other feature engineering activities. The business and data understanding are required for all forms of analytics. Using the above example, if a tabular or dashboard report is being constructed, the data scientist needs knowledge of what is needed to support earned value reporting and analysis for budgeting and cost allocation. If predictive analytics is desired, this is equally, if not more important, as assumptions will be made as these features are used in future predictions and forecasts.

Many times, the machine learning process is very exploratory in nature and once the data is prepared and analyzed, many new hypothesis and potential findings are identified. Due to this, many argue understanding the business is the most complex, compared to the Math and Programming. Said another way, Math and Programming is easy to teach and learn on a collegiate level, in a Massively Open Online Class (MOOC), or even self-taught. However, the particular business processes of a business are unique and may require many years to develop this thorough understanding. Therefore, the data scientist will often rely on the business analyst to assist.

Once the business understanding and problem definition is captured, then the data scientist can begin the exploratory activity to identify what data may be useful to meet the identified goals.

PREPARE DATA

Data preparation is the agglomeration of collecting, cleaning, adjusting, and preprocessing the data to be used in the subsequent activities. This data enrichment ensures the data is transformed to meet the goals of the particular following activities. Considerations include inconsistencies in data, missing data, various formats, adjusting normality, etc. Data preparation may occur within a combination of Extract, Translate, & Load (ETL) tools (e.g., SQL Server Integration Services, Informatica, etc.), self-service data prep (e.g., Alteryx, Excel, etc.), or data science tools (e.g., R, Python, SAS, etc.).

Predictive algorithms generally want the maximum prediction power from the fewest variables. This assists with avoiding the curse of dimensionality and ensures proper fitting (note: this varies by algorithm but stands in a general sense). Also, the algorithm would likely learn/run faster with fewer variables.

The following are some of the activities that occur during this phase:

- ETL cleansing and furnishing. Traditional ETL assumes data originates at various sources and will be transformed prior to being furnished to a destination. This may include using master tables for lookups, combining various formats (e.g., varchar(10) vs.

nvarchar(10), etc.). These tasks are often conducted by data engineers, although it is very useful for data scientists to be aware of these activities.

- Exploratory Data Analysis. Exploratory Data Analysis (EDA) is likely one of the first steps a data scientist conducts in order to orient themselves to the new dataset. Some Techniques include:

  o Utilize clustering to evaluate potential groupings via K-means, DBSCAN, or Hierarchal clustering. This assists with hypothesis development and identifying potential questions to be evaluated.

  o Univariate, bivariate, and multivariate analysis with summary statistics across input features of interest. These simple techniques are often useful to determine valuable relationships and behaviors.

- Determine if correlated variables exist and how to handle, such as Pearsons, Anova, LDA, Chi-Squared, etc. based on if the variables are continuous or categorical. In most machine learning algorithms, highly correlated variables lead to overfitting and should be dealt with by removing or using a dimension reduction technique (to be covered later).

- Determine outlier treatment. Most machine learning algorithms are sensitive to the range of distribution, so handling outliers generally has a large impact on improving your model. Possible resolution could be deletion or imputation (such as with the mean). Binning may also reduce the variance caused by outliers. Additionally, rather than immediately disregarding, outliers can provide deep insight into other areas of exploration.

- Determine missing value treatment. Deleting the row is an option, but then we may miss out on valuable information from the other input features. Imputing the Mean, Mode, or Median (depending if quantitative or qualitative attributes) is also common.

- Feature Engineering allows us to create new features based on characteristics of the data, such as derived columns, combined columns, or calculated columns.

- Encoding data. Some models require or perform better with encoded data. For example, one-hot encoding to convert categorical features to Boolean columns by category so they perform better in the subsequent modeling phase.

- Transforming data to adjust to normality. Examples include evaluating skewness to determine if transforms are needed (e.g., log transforms, multiplicative inverse, etc.).

- Imbalanced Data. This common issue involves having classes that are not represented equally (e.g., for example 95% of the data is 'Yes' and 5% is 'No'). Four common techniques are used with this approach, which include under-sampling the majority class, oversampling the minority class, generate synthetic records (e.g., SMOTE – a favorite of mine), and using cost sensitive models that penalize the classification based on the minority observation. One of the most critical aspects of imbalanced data is to use the proper evaluation technique. For instance, accuracy should not be used on imbalanced classes, rather confusion matrix, F1, precision, recall, etc.

Data preparation is likely one of the most important steps in a data science project. Algorithms make assumptions about the data, which must be considered. Additionally, the results can likely be improved by using proper preparation techniques. The previous section identifies some common techniques. Additional techniques exist that are a bit more complex and exotic and may be used if we are trying to tweak a bit more performance from our model. However, we must balance the effort with the reward. For instance, is an extra 80hrs of work worth a slight improvement? In some scenarios yes, in others, no.

From a data preparation vantage, there is no single set of techniques that can be used in all scenarios, given each dataset and goal is different. Establishing your own techniques will be useful to build confidence in how you can approach your next project. And, as with anything, practice and exploring is the best approach to refining your techniques.

MODELING

Modeling is typically segregated into supervised and unsupervised learning. Supervised learning utilizes labeled data that identifies a desired outcome and the impact of input columns on that output. This allows supervised algorithms to utilize probability to make predictions about future scenarios on unseen data. Unsupervised learning attempts to find patterns of commonality.

Unsupervised Machine Learning is a group of algorithms and approaches that use unlabeled data. Essentially, what this means is there is no column or feature that has the correct answer from past observations. Compared to supervised learning, we do have a labeled outcome or dependent variable, with input features or independent variables that try to predict the labeled outcome or dependent variable.

Unsupervised learning is very useful in three primary areas, which include clustering, association rules, and dimension reduction. Clustering is the most widely used category of unsupervised learning. Association Rules and Dimension Reduction will be covered later in the book. Clustering is very useful to assist us with making recommendations as well as hypothesis development for subsequent tasks, such as supervised learning.

The first use of clustering originated in the 1850s in London, when John Snow used spatial clustering of cholera deaths around the broad street water pump. Similarly, clustering has many uses within common business scenarios, which will be covered in the algorithm section of this book.

Supervised differs from unsupervised in that prior data includes a predictor field that is labeled. Said another way, we have historical observations that we are attempting to derive patterns. This is similar to using the traditional scientific method where we derive a causal diagram. Similar to this causal diagram, supervised machine learning algorithms attempt to find input features that predict an outcome. This is done by using input features as independent variables and evaluating their relationship and predictive power to the dependent variable or output variable. Consider the following diagram that illustrates a theoretical model of customer satisfaction for a product. We may have data for four columns, which would include quality, cost, features, and customer satisfaction. These columns could be categorial or numerical. For instance, quality could be: low, medium, and high. Cost would be of numerical in type, and features could also be numerical. Customer satisfaction may be represented as a categorical value, such as low, medium, or high or even using something such as a Likert Scale on a 1-5. By building a supervised algorithm, we are able to evaluate the predictive power of the three input columns to predict customer satisfaction. Doing so allows us to fine-tune our processes to increase customer satisfaction.

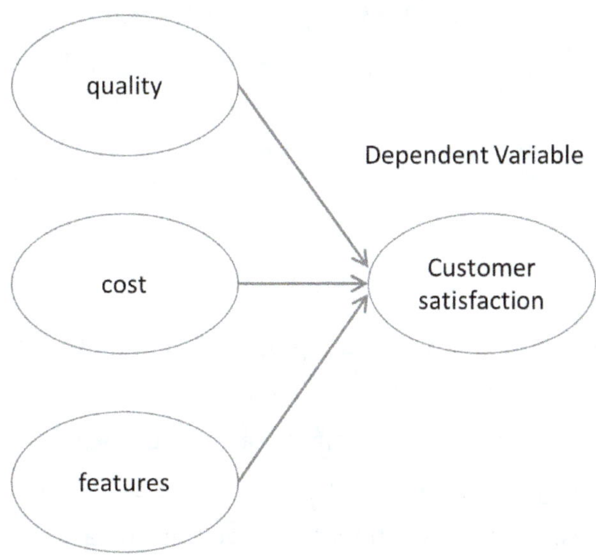

Supervised machine learning is segregated into classification and regression algorithms. The choice of which to use resides in the type of output or dependent variable being predicted. If the outcome is numerical, then a regression-based algorithm is used. If the outcome is categorical, then a classification-based algorithm is used. The following image illustrates the difference in classification and regression:

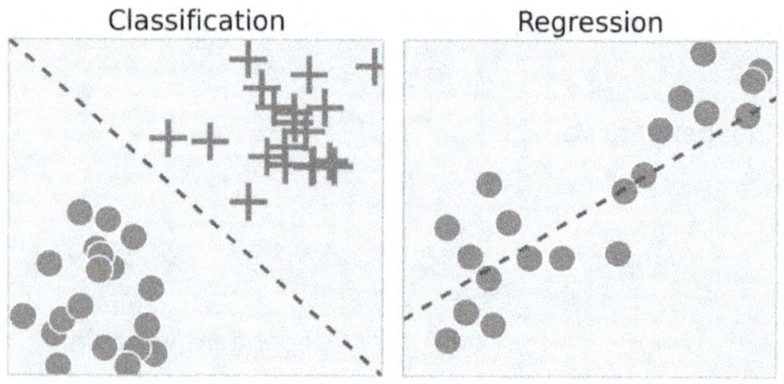

Figure 2 - Classification & Regression (Soni, 2018)

For the classification example, we can assume that we are trying to predict a dichotomous or binary outcome and in this example, has a nice linear boundary. The outcomes could be circles or crosses. Note, classifiers can have non-linear boundaries as well, which will be covered later. Our goal is to determine what input features allows us to segregate into a classification algorithm. In this example, it would classify perfect, meaning all instances clearly belong to a single class. In the real world, this is rarely the case and often some of the circles would be slightly on the crosses side and vice versa.

For the regression example, our goal is to identify a line that minimizes the vertical offsets of the instances of circles. R-Squared is often cited as the coefficient of determination that summarizes the explanatory power of the line in predicting new instances.

EVALUATE RESULTS

One of the frequent topics that emerge when discussing the results of any data science activity is if the identified correlation equals causation. It has been discussed, researched, and presented in many forms over the years. The short answer is that correlation does not always equal causation. However, sometimes, correlations are all a data science has to utilize, therefore can be informative. Consider the following diagram of ice cream sales and shark attacks. The diagram certainly shows a relationship between increased ice cream sales and shark attacks. So, if we placed in a causal diagram, would eating ice cream be a causal factor to being attacked by a shark? The only way to confirm this, as well as any causation, is with a controlled study. Doing so would identify that this relationship corollary, but it is not causal. What is missing is the confounding variable of temperature. Temperature is corollary and causal to both ice cream sales and shark attacks. As the temperature rises, more ice cream is consumed. Likewise, as the temperature rises, more people swim in the water to cool off, which places them at risk for being attacked by a shark.

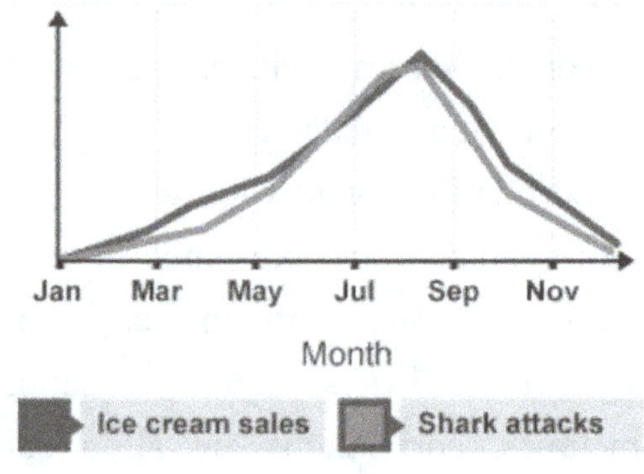

Figure 3 - Correlation vs. Causation (Cathy, 2018)

Data Scientists may not always be able to identify the confounding variable. Meaning, correlation is all that can be identified. And, this identification is nonetheless knowledge, even if causality cannot be confirmed. For instance, let us consider a common business scenario of identifying manufacturing defects. If our data shows a correlation of more defects on Friday than any other day of the week, then this is knowledge, even if we cannot identify the exact cause. Our simple action may be to just move work to other days. Or, perhaps, segregate the type of work and move complex work to earlier in the week and simpler work on Fridays. Just as with the scientific method, when hypotheses are tested, even if the hypotheses are rejected, this is still informative knowledge. Therefore, data scientists should strive to identify as much information as possible and attempt to identify both corollary and causal relationships.

The majority of business problems tend to fall into the classification space, with the exception of the financial industry.

Supervised Machine Learning segregates data into training, testing, and validation datasets to ensure that the algorithm not only identifies patterns, but generalizes well on future unseen data. Therefore, these three datasets assist with this endeavor. One simple, yet common approach is to use a 70% training, 15% testing, and 15% validation. Using this approach, an algorithm is developed using the training dataset, then applied to the testing segment. Feedback is included from testing to evolve the algorithm. Once this feedback has been included, the validation dataset can be used to evaluate how well the algorithm will generalize on future data. While some utilize a 70% training and 30% testing, this may introduce the risk of proper fitting by placing too much emphasis on the testing feedback. The goal of training is to identify the best fit of the data and avoid underfitting and overfitting. The following diagram illustrates proper fitting:

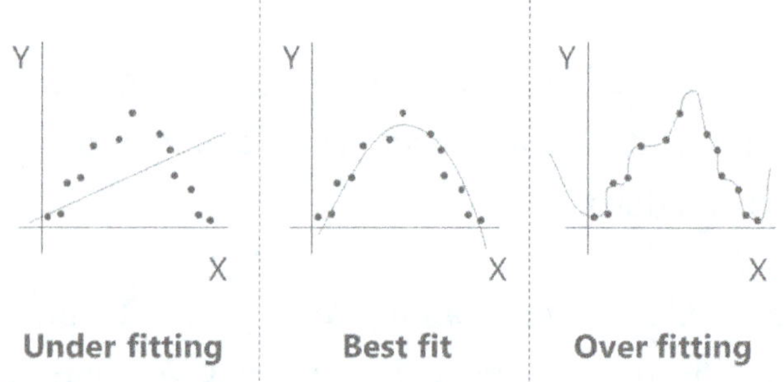

As discussed previously, predictive machine learning algorithms fall within two categories – regression and classification. In the majority of scenarios, classification is used more frequently. Each utilize different evaluation metrics.

For classification algorithms, the Area Under the Receiver Operating Characteristic (ROC) Curve, or often called the AUC and an error matrix are the two commonly used evaluation metrics. Of these two, the error matrix and sometimes called the confusion matrix is most easy to communicate, especially with a binary outcome. With many outcomes, the term confusion may come to fruition, given the complexity of the chart. The following is an example of a binary error matrix:

N=165	Actual: Yes		Actual: No	
Predicted: Yes	TP	100	FP	10
Predicted: No	FN	5	TN	50

In this example, we have a total of 165 predictions. 110 of these were predicted as 'Yes' and 55 as 'No'. However, in reality, we have 105 as 'Yes' and 60 as 'No'. In this chart "TP" stands for True Positive, "FP" stands for False Positive, "FN" stands for False Negative, and "TN" stands for True Negative. Our goal is to have high True Positives and True Negatives and Low False Positives and False Negatives. We can use this matrix when we apply our algorithm to our training and validation dataset. If we see a high False Positive and False Negative, we can use that feedback to adjust our algorithm.

Assuming this error matrix is from our testing dataset, a few other metrics exist, which include: Accuracy, Precision, Recall, and F-Score.

Accuracy provides an overall view of how often the classifier is correct. The calculation for Accuracy is (TP+TN/Total), which equals (100+50)/165=0.91. One potential risk with using accuracy alone is to consider the balance of the predicted variable. For instance, if the testing dataset has 90% yes as TP and 10% no as TN, then we could just have our algorithm predict Yes 100% of the time and be 0.90 correct. Therefore, accuracy is not useful when we have class imbalances such as this. For these scenarios, other metrics are more useful.

Precision provides information for when it predicts yes, how often the prediction is correct. The calculation is TP/Predicted Yes, which equals (100/110)=0.91.

Recall provides us with how many of the predictions are actually correct. The calculation for recall is TP/(TP+FN), which equates to 100/(100+5)=0.95.

F-Score provide a general recommendation on how good the model is at predicting an outcome and being correct. It is also useful for class imbalances. The F-Score calculation is 2(Precision*Recall)/(Precision+Recall), which equates to 0.93. An F-Score of 1.0 is the best value, which means we have a perfect precision and recall.

The ROC can be drawn with the FP rate on the X-axis and the TP rate on the Y-axis, such as the below:

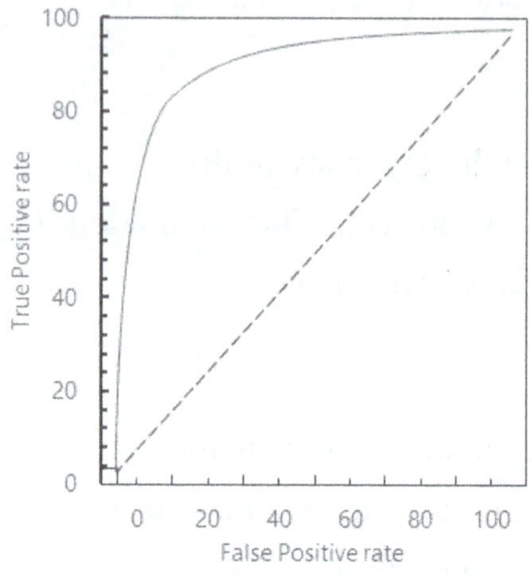

Careful consideration should be taken when the results of a model are presented. F-Scores and ROC Curves provide a good representation to how well a model generalizes on unseen data, even with unbalanced classes. In the case of imbalanced classes, if the classes are adjusted to be more balanced using under-sampling or over-sampling, then other measures, such as accuracy may be useful.

COMMUNICATE RESULTS

Communicating the results is often one of the most challenging aspects of a data science project. Many see this as the reason why a particular model or activity fails to be successful. This arises from the ability to communicate the complexity of modeling to a broad audience range, such as highly technical through executive leadership/management.

Many techniques can be used, such as proper visualization, knowing how to read the non-verbal or body language of the audience so adjustments can be made, and ensuring the proper model is used that balances the ability to communicate versus the amount of accuracy. For instance, a decision tree is very easy to communicate compared to an Artificial Neural Network (ANN). Even though the ANN may be slightly more accurate, the decision tree approach may be easier to communicate, convince, and adopt.

Knowing the proper visualization technique is critical to ensuring the proper message is created and communicated. The following diagrams provides common guidance for establishing the communication goals and guiding on which to use (Seif, 2018).

Comparison (Among Items & One-Time):

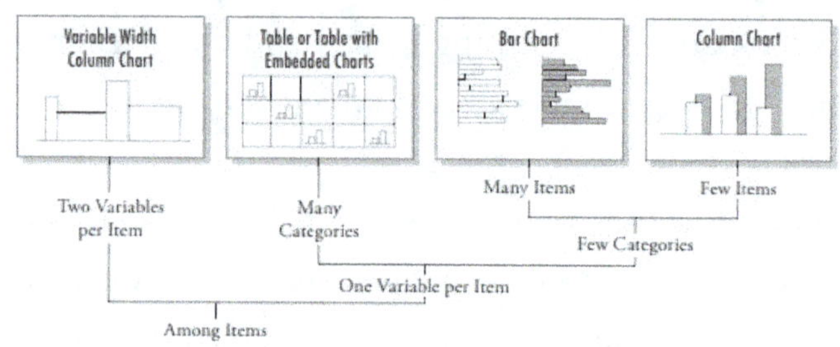

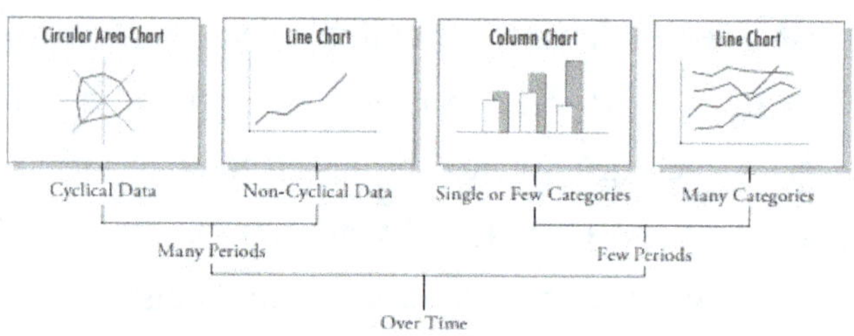

Distribution:

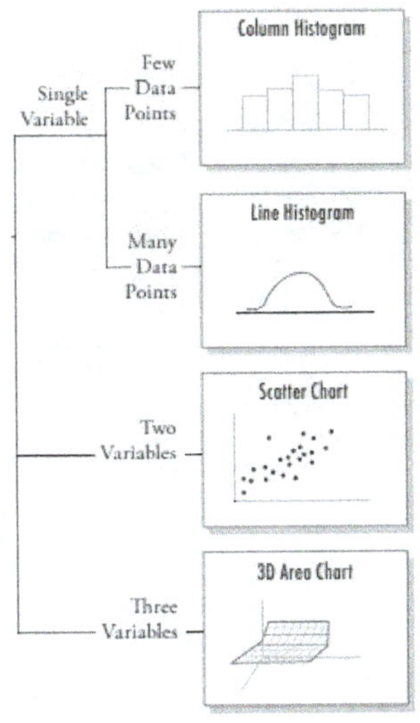

Composition (Static & Changing over Time):

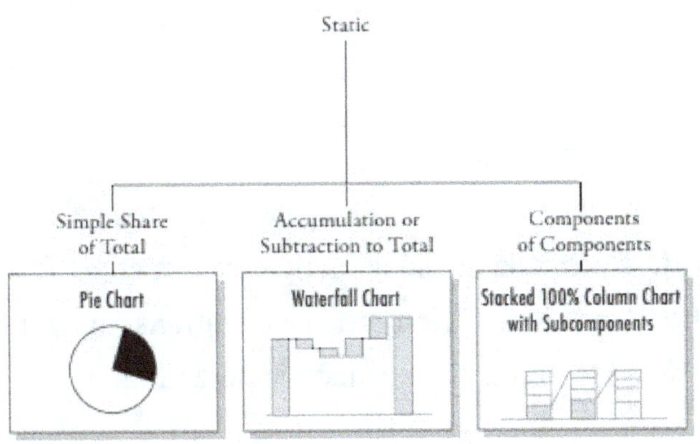

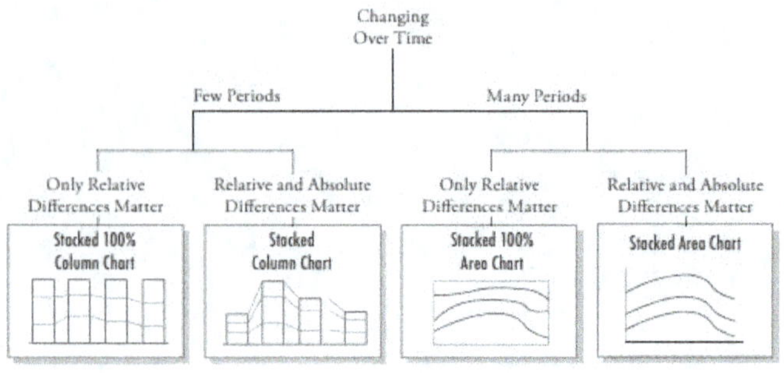

Relationship:

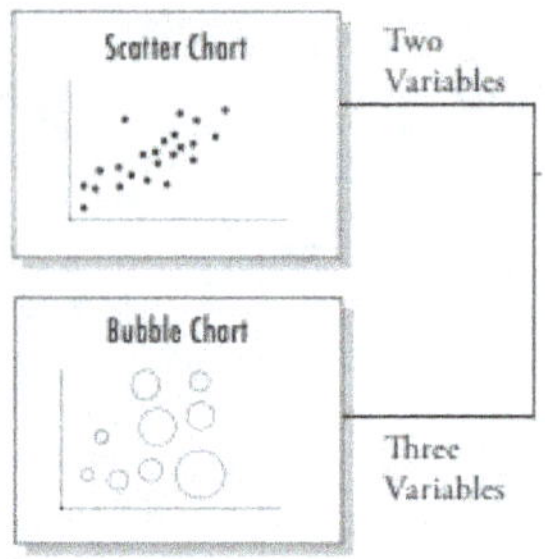

Through the use of this guidance, the proper libraries in the data science languages, such as R or Python, which are rich in visualizations, may be leveraged to create the needed visualization.

The role of communication is studied and applied in all aspects of a professional and personal setting.

However, through utilizing best practices, a Data Scientist is able to leverage these techniques to their advantage. Albert Mehrabian, a professor of Psychology at UCLA, is world renown for his research and publications on the importance of verbal and non-verbal communication. His research shows that 7% of communication is spoken words, 38% is voice/tone, and 55% is body language (Belludi, 2008). The following diagram illustrates the many considerations to utilize on both sides of communication:

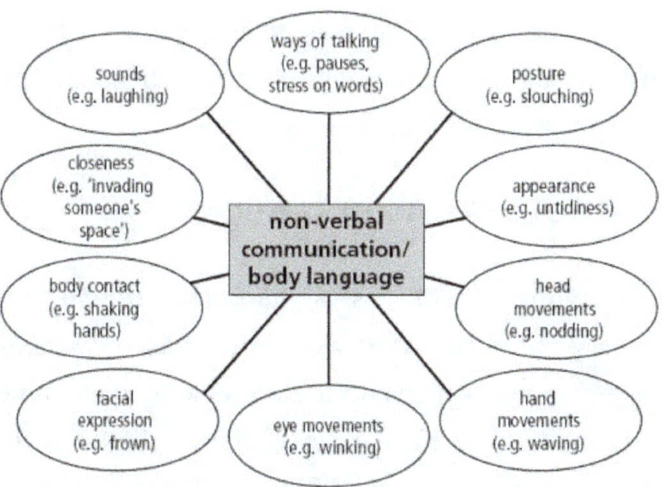

As a Data Scientist, knowing how to adjust the presentation or communication that leverages these techniques can be the difference between success and failure.

Often, the type of model used may sacrifice some accuracy for better communication results. An example may be using a simple Decision Tree algorithm, which is relatively easy to communicate versus Support Vector Machines, which is a bit more complex. When presenting to an executive who many have little experience with Data Science, it may be advantageous to utilize a slightly less accurate model over a complex one to ensure proper understanding. This understanding can be the difference between moving forward to the next step, which would be model deployment.

THE ROLE OF STORYTELLING

Storytelling establishes a narrative around the visuals and data. What would otherwise be a non-engaging and perhaps boring presentation can come to life with some simple Storytelling techniques. In the figure below, Dykes (2016) combines Narrative, Visuals, and Data To establish the ability to explain, enlighten, and engage. The synthesis of these activities allows for change to occur.

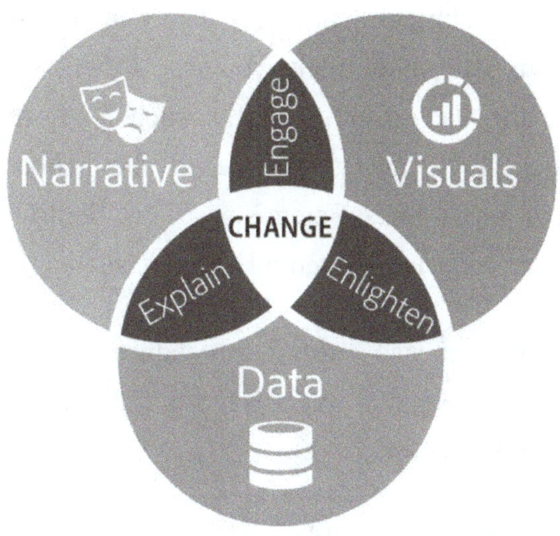

The research of Antonio Damosio, who is a professor of neuroscience at USC, found that decisions are based on emotion more so than simple logic (Damosio, 2009). Therefore, engagement and emotional connection may be established to help with the needed influence on organizational change.

DEPLOYMENT

From a technical vantage, deployment of an algorithm can take many routes. Often, it will require the use of other skills, such as Software Engineering, which is outside of the scope and skills of most Data Scientists. This deployment may occur via many potential options, such as:

- A database stored procedure, which is included with vendors such as Microsoft SQL Server.

- A web-based API.

- An interactive Application.

Deployment is a very immature area of Data Science. Many vendors take various approaches. For instance, RStudio utilizes Connect and Shiny to publish algorithms and build full-stack applications in only the R language. This architecture allows for the RStudio Client to publish directly to the RStudio Server Infrastructure. For the Python language, Anaconda is widely used and has deployment options for interactive Python applications, APIs, and the use of simple reports. Architecturally, this is similar to RStudio. Others may choose to be agnostic to a particular platform and utilize neutral languages such as Microsoft .NET, Java, and/or JavaScript to build an application that executes the model. These may use their internal libraries for modeling or execute R or Python as needed.

With deployment, new records may be "scored" interactively or in a batch-type model. From an interactive perspective, this may occur when new data is created and a prediction is needed. From a batch perspective, an accumulation of data may be created and a set time (e.g., 8pm nightly) may be used to score the accumulated data.

Once the new data is scored, then the information can be placed in the hands of knowledge workers to utilize the prediction. Or, the use of prescriptive analytics may utilize autonomy to make the decision without a human-in-the-loop. An emerging approach is to integrate these predictions with Robotic Process Automation (RPA). RPA is a new technology that automates workflows within an employee's common computing activity. For instance, if a mundane and repetitive task such as opening email, opening attachment, reading data, adding two columns from a spreadsheet, etc., this can be replaced with essentially an automated macro – hence the term Robotic Process Automation. Future use of RPA will combine these mundane tasks with prescriptive analytics for optimized business processes.

Types of Machine Learning

UNSUPERVISED LEARNING

From a theoretical vantage, Unsupervised Machine Learning was the first type of learning to be applied. An early example is the 1854 cholera outbreak in London. During this outbreak, physician John Snow developed a hypothesis that water was the causal factor. Using a mapping mechanism, such as the below, this was tested and found to be the underlying cause (Rosenberg, 2014).

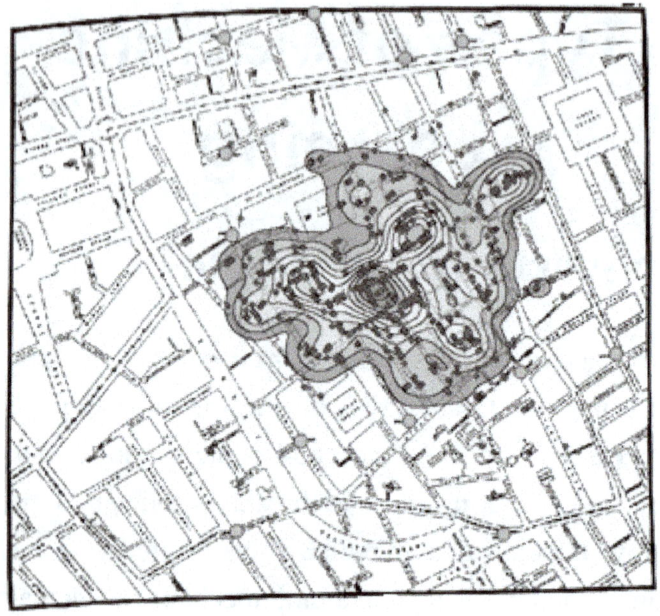

Using a mapping mechanism such as the above, Snow was able to trace the cause to a water well. This essentially extracts patterns from data without labels. Said another way, all the cases of "true" and "false" can be segmented so that a pattern can be extracted from those who hold the "true" attribute of being infected with the disease.

Another example of unsupervised learning is the ability to draw inferences and make recommendations. In the example below, we have the height and weight of a population and are able to infer spherical clusters based on the sizes of small, medium, and large (Peterson, 2018). This dataset is nice and clean with no outliers, that would likely exist in a real dataset. Therefore, data prep to remove or address prior may be needed.

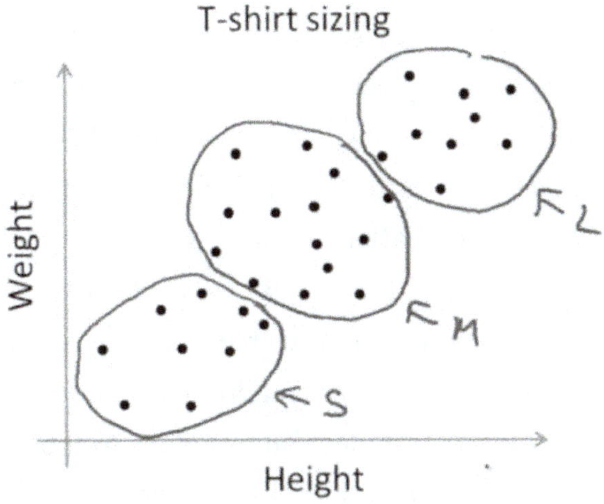

As we can see in this example, an unsupervised algorithm attempts to infer clusters of observations that infer a recommendation. In this scenario, we do not have prior labeled examples of Small, Medium, and Large. Rather, we infer this recommendation.

SUPERVISED LEARNING

Supervised learning is categorized as two types: regression and classification. The type is dictated by the predictor variable and if this variable is continuous (e.g., numeric) or categorical/discreet. Examples of continuous would be dollar amounts, hours, ages, number of wins vs. loses, etc. Examples of categorical/discreet would be: color choice (e.g., red, green, blue), gender, city, etc. In supervised learning, we leverage pre-labeled data that defines the correct output in the training set. This set is created after the raw data is prepared for use via feature extraction, quality checks, dimension reduction, and many other techniques. For instance, if the data has dozens or hundreds of columns, we may use dimension reduction to reduce to those that are the most influential. This concept will be covered in detail later. Or, if missing values or outliers are present, those may need attention, depending on the algorithm to be used. Some algorithms are sensitive to outliers and missing values and some are not. Once the raw data is prepped, the labels can be created and/or identified. This is simply identifying the column that has the labels.   Next the actual modeling can occur. Common supervised algorithms are included in the following two tables:

Algorithm	Problem Type	Results interpretable by you?	Easy to explain algorithm to others?	Average predictive accuracy	Training speed
KNN	Either	Yes	Yes	Lower	Fast
Linear regression	Regression	Yes	Yes	Lower	Fast
Logistic regression	Classification	Somewhat	Somewhat	Lower	Fast
Naive Bayes	Classification	Somewhat	Somewhat	Lower	Fast (excluding feature extraction)
Decision trees	Either	Somewhat	Somewhat	Lower	Fast
Random Forests	Either	A little	No	Higher	Slow
AdaBoost	Either	A little	No	Higher	Slow
Neural networks	Either	No	No	Higher	Slow

Algorithm	Prediction speed	Amount of parameter tuning needed (excluding feature selection)	Performs well with small number of observations?	Handles lots of irrelevant features well (separates signal from noise)?	Automatically learns feature interactions?	Parametric?
KNN	Depends on n	Minimal	No	No	No	No
Linear regression	Fast	None (excluding regularization)	Yes	No	No	Yes
Logistic regression	Fast	None (excluding regularization)	Yes	No	No	Yes
Naive Bayes	Fast	Some for feature extraction	Yes	Yes	No	Yes
Decision trees	Fast	Some	No	No	Yes	No
Random Forests	Moderate	Some	No	Yes (unless noise ratio is very high)	Yes	No
AdaBoost	Fast	Some	No	Yes	Yes	No
Neural networks	Fast	Lots	No	Yes	Yes	No

REINFORCED LEARNING

A third category of machine learning algorithms emerges when an algorithm can assess the environment and make adjustments to maximize the gain and benefit, as well as learn from mistakes. This is often referred to as reinforced learning. Forster (2014) described the three categories of machine learning as illustrated below:

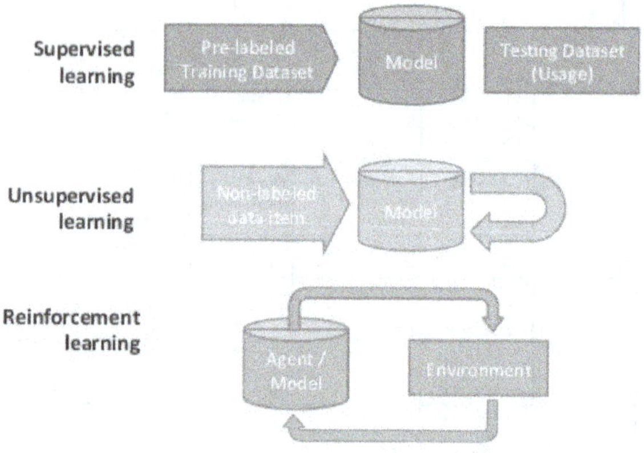

As shown in this diagram, reinforced learning is similar to supervised learning. However, a Data Scientist does not use training/testing/validation data to create and publish the model. Rather, an agent with a reward system is defined. For instance, consider a Roomba Vacuum system. The Roomba navigates our living spaces and constantly bumps into objects, such as chairs, walls, doors, etc. As the device bumps into obstructions, it will take another route and attempt to avoid what it has learned is an object in the past. These devices now include applications on smart devices to even customize the map or tell the device to "Clean the Kitchen". Through this reward system, the device can now operate in this environment.

TIME-SERIES

The final category of Machine Learning Algorithms is time-series. Within this category, the goal is to predict an outcome, but considers the basis of time to infer a prediction or forecast. Time-Series algorithms attempt to draw conclusions of prior history and determine if a trend can be identified. For instance, in the housing market, we can evaluate if home prices per square foot are increasing or decreasing, based on a set of historical observations. Additionally, seasonality may also be utilized to assist in fine-tuning the algorithm. An example of this may be online retail and the spike of Holiday Shopping.

The Unsupervised Learning Toolbox

CLUSTERING

Clustering is the largest category of unsupervised learning. Many see these terms as analogous. However, there are other unsupervised approaches, which will also be covered in this section. Clustering is often performed prior to any supervised learning as an exploratory approach to either gain a better understanding of the data or help develop hypotheses that can later be evaluated in a supervised manner.

Quite simply, clustering is the simple process of combining common entities together. Doing so provides insight into underlying patterns that may otherwise not be recognizable. The common techniques of K-Means Clustering, Density-Based

Clustering (DBSCAN), and Hierarchical Clustering will be covered. While this list is not exhaustive, it does cover the most commonly used techniques.

K-MEANS CLUSTERING

K-Means Clustering is a technique that tries to generate k clusters where each object belongs to a cluster with the nearest mean. When executed, we simply provide k to our dataset and the goal is to maximize inter-cluster variance and minimize intra-cluster variance (e.g., small tight circles far away from one another where the number of circles equals k). K-Means clustering only works with numerical data and has no notion of outliers. Meaning, otherwise good intra and inter clusters may be skewed due to outliers, therefore initial data prep may be required. Additionally, the algorithm only generates clusters that are spherical in shape. K-means also makes many iterations to converge on a good set of clusters and these cluster assignments may change on each iteration.

From a performance perspective, K-means is an efficient method of clustering. One challenge is that no widely accepted rule exists to find the optimal number of clusters. Often, it requires the comparison of multiple runs with the outcomes and different k values to determine the best results. A generally accepted rule is that a larger k probably decreases error, but leads to overfitting.

The algorithm is fairly simple and follows these steps:

1. Clusters the data into k groups where k is predefined.

2. Select k points at random as cluster centers.

3. Assign objects to their closest cluster center according to the Euclidean distance function.

4. Calculate the centroid or mean of all objects in each cluster.

5. Repeat steps 2, 3 and 4 until the same points are assigned to each cluster in consecutive rounds.

Therefore, we can derive the Pseudocode for K-Means as:

Loop through K Times
Current Centroid = Randomly Generate Values for Each Attribute
Done = False
All Instances Cluster = None
While not Done
Total Distance = 0
Done = True
For each Instance
Instance's Previous Cluster = Instance's Cluster
Measure Euclidean (or other) Distance to each Centroid
Find Smallest Distance and Assign to that Cluster
If new Cluster <> Previous Cluster
Done = False
Add Smallest Distance to Total Distance
Report Total Distance
For Each Cluster
Loop through Attributes
Loop through Instances Assigned to Cluster
Update Totals
Calculate Average for cluster = Producing new centroid
End While

The upside to K-Means Clustering is that it is very simple. The downside to K-Means clustering is it has no notion of outliers, which often skews our clusters and the results are not as accurate as we would like. Meaning, all points are assigned, even if they really are far away from the centroids.

These problematic points pull the cluster centroid towards them, making it harder to classify them as anomalous points.

One approach to dealing with outliers in K-Means is to simply remove them. However, doing so may be very time consuming, especially for a large dataset. Additionally, the removal of them may also lead to the elimination of valuable insight. Meaning, it is not rare that outliers provide deep insight into the area of research or study.

The "No Free Lunch" theorem states that no single algorithm works for all instances. Therefore, other clustering techniques should be evaluated. While K-Means is simple to use, if it does not provide the results we would like, we should evaluate other algorithms.

DBSCAN (DENSITY-BASED CLUSTERING)

Another algorithm that may be useful for unsupervised learning is DBSCAN (Density-based clustering). The primary difference is the algorithm is density-based versus centroid-based. Rather than providing k number of clusters, it infers the clusters based on the data and can discover clusters of any arbitrary shape. This overcomes another shortcoming of k-means, which infers only spherical shapes.

DBSCAN requires two parameters, which is the distance threshold epsilon and minimum number of points (MinPts).

The algorithm is fairly simple and follows these steps:

1. Start with an arbitrary seed with has at least MinPts nearby with a distance (e.g., radius of epsilon).

2. Conduct a breadth-first search along each of these nearby points.

3. For each given point, we count how many points it has within its radius, if fewer than MinPts it becomes a leaf and we do not continue to grow the cluster.

4. If the given point does have at least MinPts, it becomes a branch, and we add all of its neighbors to the First-In-First-Out (FIFO) queue of our search queue.

5. Once the breath-first search is complete, were complete with our first cluster and never revisit a point again.

6. Then we pick a new arbitrary seed point and grow the next cluster.

7. This continues until all points have been assigned.

One key aspect of DBSCAN is that if a point has fewer than MinPts and not a leaf node, it is labeled as an outlier. This is a key feature that makes DBSCAN very powerful.

Using the above steps, we can derive the Pseudocode for DBSCAN as:

```
Foreach unvisited element as P
   Mark P visited
   If P is not member of cluster
   N +=P
```

If N has more than k elements
   Add P to new cluster C
   Foreach element of N as P'
     If P is not visited
       Mark P' as visited
       N' = neighbors of P'
       If N' has more than k elements
         N+=(N+N')
      End
     End
     If P' is not a cluster member
       Add P' to cluster C
     End
   End
 Else
   P is outlier
 End
End

To summarize, DBSCAN requires two parameters, which is the distance threshold epsilon and minimum number of points (MinPts). It starts with an arbitrary seed point which has at least MinPts nearby within the distance/radius. Then we do a breadth-first search along these points. For each point, the number of points within the radius is calculated. If the results are fewer than MinPts, then it's a leaf and the cluster is not grown further. Otherwise, then the point is a branch and we add the neighbors and conduct a breadth-first search again. Once the breadth-first search is complete, the cluster is also complete and the points are never searched again. As mentioned previously, one of the interesting uses of DBSCAN is that when complete, if a point has fewer than MinPts, but not a leaf node, then it is an outlier and does not below to any cluster.

HIERARCHICAL CLUSTERING

Another popular clustering method is Hierarchical Clustering. Hierarchical clustering can occur in two ways, which is divisive (top-down) or agglomerative (bottom-up). In the divisive method, we assign all observations to a single cluster and then divide the cluster into similar and smaller clusters. This occurs recursively on each cluster until there is one cluster for each observation. In the Agglomerative method, each observation is assigned to its own cluster, then similarity or distance between observations is used to compute the most similar observations to form/merge the higher cluster. These steps occur until everything belongs to a single cluster. Both of these approaches provide a dendrogram, which is a useful visualization for evaluating the results of the clustering technique. Below is an example of a Dendrogram (What is a Dendrogram, 2018):

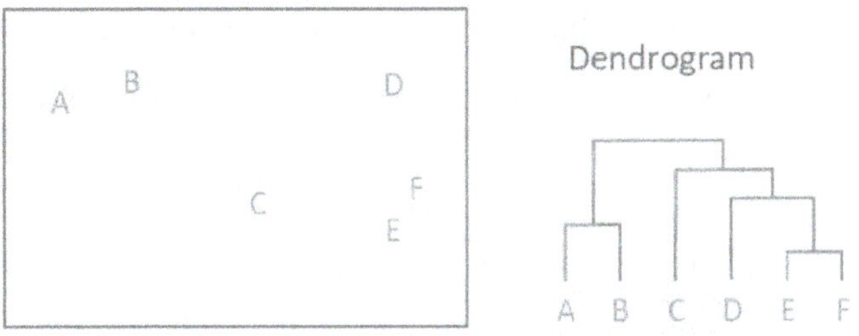

In this example we can see how circles could be applied in a top-down or bottom-sup fashion to group them. Then the chart would show the distance and relationship to one another. While the overall concept is quite simple, many different distance measures are available. These include complete linkage clustering, single linkage clustering, mean linkage clustering, and centroid linkage clustering.

- Single linkage clustering: Find the minimum possible distance between points belonging to two different clusters.

- Complete linkage clustering: Find the maximum possible distance between points belonging to two different clusters.

- Average linkage clustering: Find all possible pairwise distances for points belonging to two different clusters and then calculate the average.

- Centroid linkage clustering: Find the centroid of each cluster and calculate the distance between centroids of two clusters.

A good rule of thumb is that divisive is good for identifying large clusters while agglomerative is good for identifying small clusters. Note there are other hierarchal methods, such as Chameleon, Mean Shift, Cure, Birch, etc.

The below figure illustrates the various distance measures that are used in hierarchical clustering (Veress, 2013).

HIERARCHICAL CLUSTER DISTANCE MEASURES

Single link (nearest neighbor). The distance between two clusters is determined by the distance of the two closest objects (nearest neighbors) in the different clusters.

Complete link (furthest neighbor). The distances between clusters are determined by the greatest distance between any two objects in the different clusters (i.e., by the "furthest neighbors").

Pair-group average link. The distance between two clusters is calculated as the average distance between all pairs of objects in the two different clusters.

Pair-group centroid. The distance between two clusters is determined as the distance between centroids.

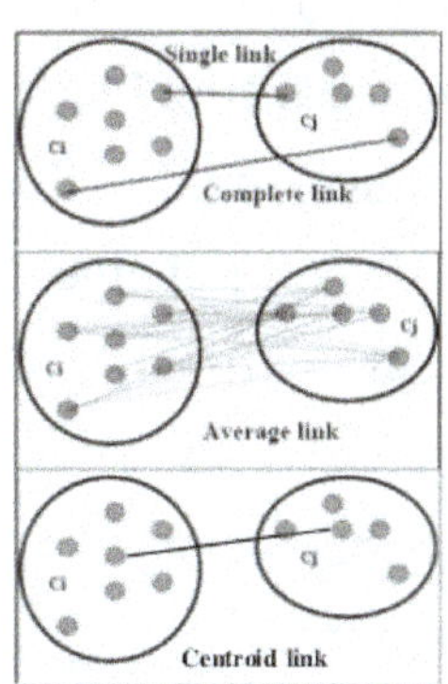

DIMENSION REDUCTION

A special case of data preparation and unsupervised learning is dimension reduction. Machine Learning algorithms typically perform better with fewer input columns. While simple data preparation techniques can reduce the features space to some extent, often, more advanced approaches such as Dimensionality Reduction is required. The underlying phenomena that first observed this need originated by Richard Bellman while researching dynamic programming/optimization. Consider the dimensionality example figure below. Let's assume our goal is to find an object hidden in the yellow boxes. With one dimension (left), this is quite easy as it is a straight line. With two dimensions, it is a bit more difficult, but achievable. With three, even more difficult. What if we have 50, 100, or 1000 dimensions? This becomes exponentially more difficult to solve. When the curse of dimensionality was defined (many decades ago), it not only referred to the large dimensional space, but the inability of the processing algorithm to scale accordingly. Some may argue that modern computers resolve this, especially considering GPU and distributed algorithms. However, the general rule that fewer dimensions are better still holds true.

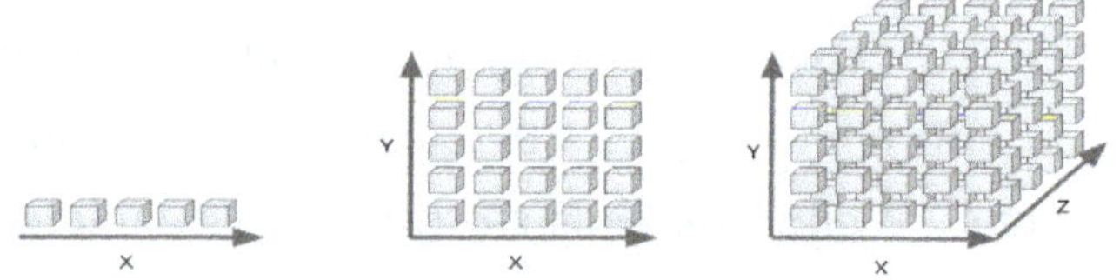

Dimension reduction techniques can be thought of as a compression of features. Said another way, these techniques combine the columns in such a way that the important features still retain meaning. Feature extraction is a popular technique that accomplishes this task. Three popular approaches to achieving this include Principle Component Analysis (PCA), Linear Discriminant Analysis (LDA), and Singular Value Decomposition (SVD).

PRINCIPLE COMPONENT ANALYSIS (PCA)

PCA is rooted deeply with linear algebra. And the fundamental notion is that the total variation of the dataset is equal to the eigenvalues and applied to eigenvectors. An eigenvector is a vector whose direction remains unchanged when a linear transformation is applied to it. An eigenvalue is the 'scalar' that is used to transform (stretch) an eigenvector. Consider the following where the red line is the eigenvector and the eigenvalues transformed the left to the right (Spruyt, 2018).

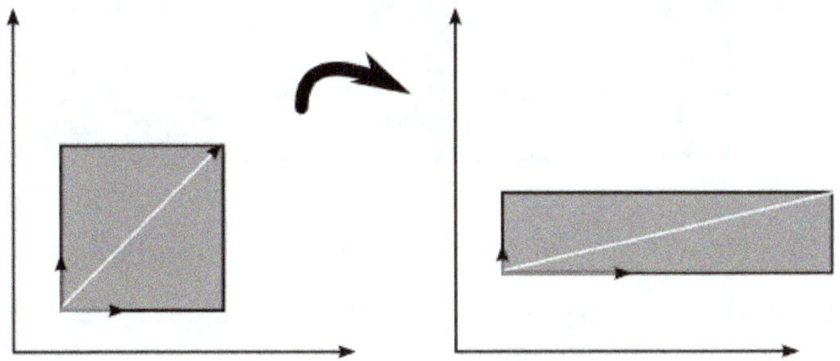

So, at a very high-level, PCA involves three steps: 1) constructing a covariance or correlation matrix (covariance if the units are of the same scale/measures and correlation for mixed), 2) compute the eigenvectors of the matrix, and 3) largest eigenvector is PC1 and explains most variation, followed by PC2 with second most, etc. The figure below illustrates a simple example of converting high-dimension to low-dimension while still retaining as much info as possible (e.g., through the rotation, we can find an optimal angle that represents the 3D version of our hand as a 2D shadow.

One final note on PCA – given the mathematics behind it, it only works on numerical data. So, if we have categorical data, we would either need to use some type of encoding (one-of-k coding) or use another technique, such as Multiple Correspondence Analysis (MCA).

LINEAR DISCRIMINANT ANALYSIS (LDA)

Linear Discriminate Analysis (LDA) is closely related to PCA, with the main difference being that it requires numerical input features/independent variables and a categorical predictor/dependent variable. It is commonly used as a data preprocessing step in classification scenarios. Compared to PCA, LDA attempts to find a linear combination of these input features, while also separating two or more classes. So, we could think of PCA as only trying to find the component axes, while LDA does this as well as maximizing the separation between classes. Discriminant analysis is used to determine which features discriminate between two or more naturally occurring groups. It accomplishes this via finding boundaries around the clusters of classes and then projects the data points along this line so the clusters are separated as much as possible. This allows LDA to be used as both a dimension reduction technique as well as a supervised classification algorithm. The figure below illustrates this difference (Raschka, 2014):

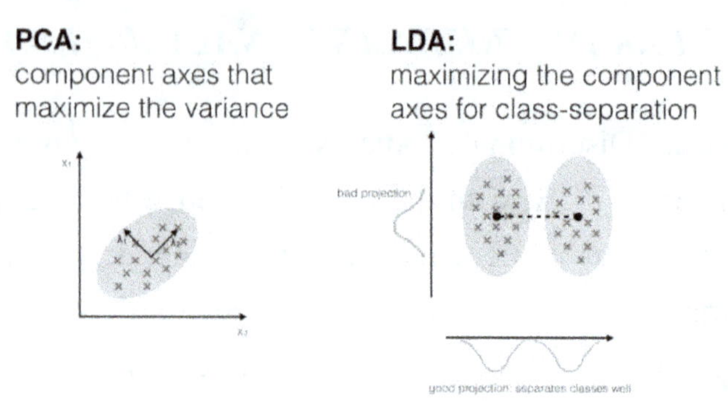

SINGULAR VALUE DECOMPOSITION (SVD)

Singular Value Decomposition (SVD), also heavily relying on linear algebra, is a method that provides a convenient method for breaking a matrix into smaller and more meaningful pieces. Matrix multiplication is used to transform the data in a way that reduces the input feature space. SVD is applied to square matrices (singular matrices) that do not have inverses. SVD can be broken into two major steps: 1) convert/reduce the initial matrix using householder transform (reflection), and 2) to create a diagonalized matrix using orthogonal transforms (rotation).

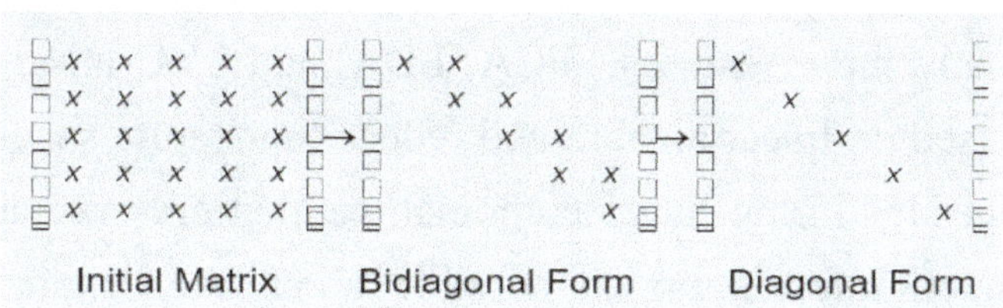

Figure 4 - SVD Transforms

UNSUPERVISED DEEP LEARNING

One of the exciting areas of Deep Learning (e.g, Artificial Intelligence) is the notion that the curse of dimensionality does not apply or is lessoned, compared to traditional Machine Learning approaches. The previously mentioned reduction techniques utilize linear methods. Autoencoders are relatively new area of deep learning that is technically an unsupervised dimension reduction technique that uses neural networks to reduce a non-linear dimensional space.

As mentioned previously, classical machine learning algorithms generally perform better with fewer input features. The curse of dimensionality provides the underlying theory for why this is true – in addition to some algorithm's overfitting with too many input features. PCA, LDA, and SVD all are based on linear algebra and reduce the feature space via identifying linear combinations that preserve as much information as possible about the original input features. Using these techniques can assist with improving model performance, so are good techniques to have in your data science toolbox.

ASSOCIATION RULES

Association rules are also a popular and widely used area of unsupervised learning. Many see this as analogous with Market Basket Analysis as it is heavily used in retail and similar scenarios. For instance, if someone purchases baby diapers, what is the probability of other related items, such as baby food. So, we can see this as a simple approach to determining if X and Y occur together.

Association rules can measure the association by three approaches, which include support,

104

confidence, and lift. Support measures the popularity of an itemset by the proportion of transactions in which an itemset appears. Confidence measures how likely item Y is purchased when item X is purchased, expressed as {X -> Y}. This is calculated by the proportion of transactions with item X, in which item Y also appears. Lift evaluates how likely item Y is purchased when item X is purchased, while controlling for the popularity of Y. A lift value greater than 1 means that item Y is likely to be bought if item X is bought, while a value less than 1 means that item Y is unlikely to be bought if item X is bought.

The following table illustrates these three measures (Sayad, 2019).

Rule	Support	Confidence	Lift
$A \Rightarrow D$	2/5	2/3	10/9
$C \Rightarrow A$	2/5	2/4	5/6
$A \Rightarrow C$	2/5	2/3	5/6
$B \& C \Rightarrow D$	1/5	1/3	5/9

These can be calculated as:

$$Support = \frac{frq(X,Y)}{N}$$

$$Rule:\ X \Rightarrow Y$$

$$Confidence = \frac{frq(X,Y)}{frq(X)}$$

$$Lift = \frac{Support}{Supp(X) \times Supp(Y)}$$

Using these approaches, organizations can apply these measures to all products they offer. Then incentives can be offered, which appeal to customers. The challenge is this can be computationally expensive. Especially with a large catalog of items.

The Supervised Learning Toolbox

TRAINING AND GENERALIZATION

As discussed in the Data Science process section, the goal of a Supervised Algorithm is to develop a model that can be applied to new and unseen data. This is often called generalization – meaning, how well the model 'Generalizes' on future data. This relates to the discussion on underfitting, overfitting, and finding the best fit.

Two approaches are used for training and generalization, which include a simple hold-out and cross-validation. The hold-out approach was discussed previously and uses three portions for training, validation, and testing. The benefit is that training occurs very quickly with less computation than k-fold. The downside is that the training is subject to higher variance given the smaller size of the data. The below illustrates the Holdout approach (Kelley, 2017):

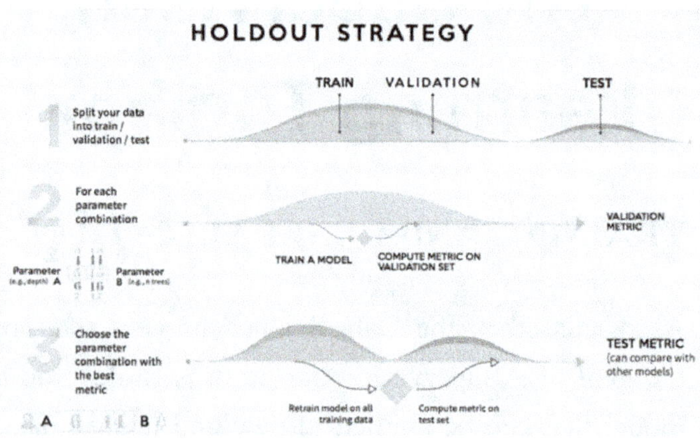

K-fold validation is similar, but evaluates the data across the entire training set by dividing the training set into K folds. Then, the model is trained K times, each time leaving a different fold out of the training data and using it instead as a validation set. Generally speaking, K-Fold tends to provide better results as it is less prone to variation since the entire training set is used (e.g., larger population). However, K-Fold is computationally expensive as the model is trained K times. The following diagram illustrates K-Fold (Kelley, 2017):

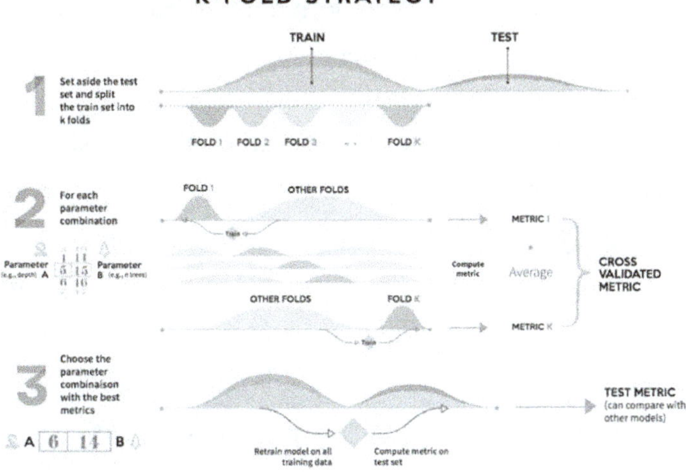

REGRESSION ALGORITHMS AND ITS VARIANTS

Linear regression is a widely used approach of predicting numerical outcomes. It originates in statistics, but is also heavily used in Machine Learning. One variable is considered the explanatory variable (e.g., predictor variable(s) of X) and the other is the dependent variable (e.g., a target variable of Y) so that a regression line can form the equation $Y = a + bX$, where b is the slope and a is the intercept. However, before using, there must be a linear relationship between the variables X and Y. Otherwise, other types of regressions may be better suited, such as Polynomial, Ridge, Lasso, etc, which are a bit more complex.

A Linear regression model is based on several assumptions, which include the errors being normally distributed with a zero mean and a constant variance. Provided the assumptions are satisfied, the regression estimators are optimal in the sense that they are unbiased, efficient, and consistent. Unbiased means that the expected value of the estimator is equal to the true value of the parameter. Efficient means that the estimator has a smaller variance than any other estimator. Consistent means that the bias and variance of the estimator approach zero as the sample size approaches infinity.

Linear Regression is often based on the ordinary least squares (OLS) approach so that the model is fit such that the sum-of-squares of differences of observed and predicted values is minimized. In Ordinary Least Squares (OLS) Linear Regression, our goal is to find the line (or hyperplane) that minimizes the vertical offsets. Or, in other words, we define the best-fitting line as the line that minimizes the sum of squared errors (SSE) or mean squared error (MSE) between our target variable (Y) and our predicted output over all samples i in our dataset of size n. OLS can be visualized as the below (Raschka, 2018).

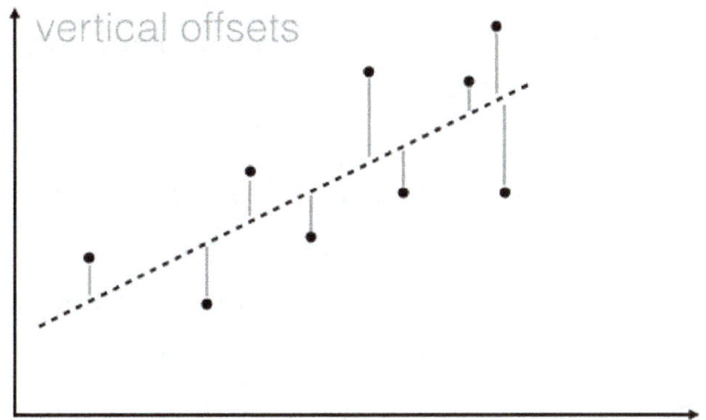

With the goal of minimizing the offsets, we can determine the intercept on the Y-Axis and angle/slope of the line.

The R-Squared or R^2 is often cited as the measure of model performance. R^2 also called as coefficient of determination summarizes the explanatory power of the regression model and is computed from the sums-of-squares terms. R^2 describes the proportion of variance of the dependent variable explained by the regression model. If the regression model is 'perfect', the R^2 is 1. If the regression model is a total failure, the R^2 is zero. It is important to keep in mind that there is no direct relationship between high R^2 and causation. Meaning, correlation does not imply causation as discussed previously.

The Pseudocode for Regression involves four steps:

1) The first step is to use the training data to calculate the mean and variance of the X and Y variables. The mean from the list of inputs is simply the mean(n) = sum(n) / count(n). The variance is the sum((n-mean(n))^2). These values will be used in the following step.

2) Next, we calculate covariance, which is simple a measure of correlation. Since correlation can be defined as the relationship between two groups of numbers, covariance can describe the relationship between two or more groups of numbers. Meaning, it describes how those two groups change together. We can calculate covariance between the two variables as sum((x(i) -

mean(x)) * (y(i) - mean(y))), where i is all observations.

3) The third step involves estimating the coefficients for the intercept and the slope. The slope b can be calculated as covariance(x, y) / variance(x) and the intercept a can be calculated as mean(y) - b * mean(x). The Intercept controls the starting point of the line where it intercepts the Y-Axis and the Slope is the amount that the Y variable will change for each 1 unit change in the X variable.

4) To utilize in machine learning, linear regression utilizes the coefficients identified in the training dataset and applying to either a testing/validation set or a future unseen dataset, depending on the goal. The equation to apply is quite simple and is: $y = n + b * x$.

Linear regression has many assumptions that must be met in order for the approach to predict well. First, the relationship between x and y should be linear. Second, it requires all variables to be multivariate normal distribution. Third, there should be little to no multicollinearity within the data. Multicollinearity means the independent variables are too highly correlated with one another. A simple correlation matrix is used to identify such scenarios. Many agree that a correlation over 0.90 is high enough to simply drop. However, other metrics, such as the Variance Inflation Factor (VIF), is needed in more complex scenarios. Fourth, there should be little to no autocorrelation of the data. Autocorrelation occurs when the residuals are not independent from each other. Lastly, it assumes the analysis is homoscedasticity, which means the residuals are equal across the regression line.

Regression models can be validated by reviewing the residuals. These are the difference between the observed value of y and the predicted value of y. Using the residuals, we can not only check the assumptions of the linear regression, but it allows us to improve the model in an exploratory approach. Basically, if you can detect a clear pattern or trend in your residuals, then your model has room for improvement. An example of reviewing the residuals is below (Bommae, 2015):

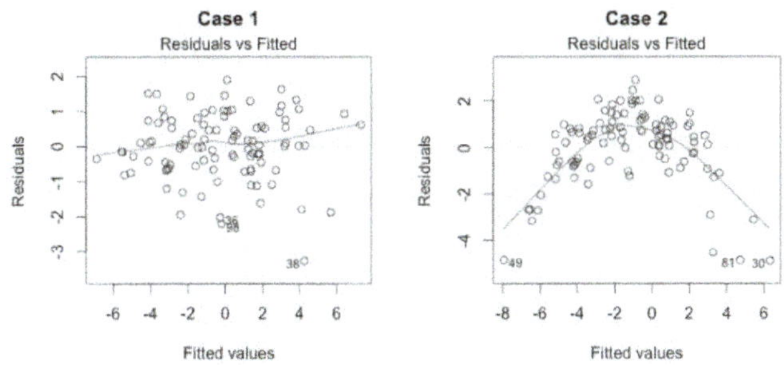

The first assumption we can validate is if the relationship is linear. Using the above, we are evaluating if the plot has a non-linear pattern. If you find equally spread residuals around a horizontal line without distinct patterns, that is a good indication you don't have non-linear relationships. The left has no clear patterns, while the right has a Parabola. So the Parabola would have opportunities to improve via the use of non-linear regression approaches.

The second assumption we can validate is if the residuals is normally distributed. Q-Q Plots are also used to show if residuals are normally distributed. In the diagram below, the left shows a model that is normally distributed. The right shows a model that has opportunity to improve.

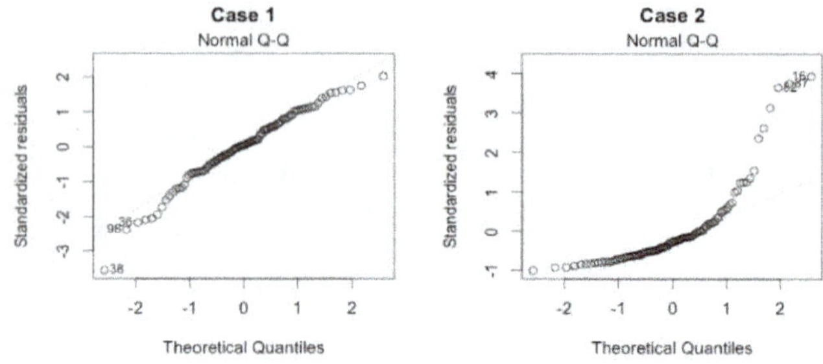

The third assumption we can validate is if homoscedasticity is present. For this we use the Scale-Location plot. This plot shows if residuals are spread equally along the ranges of predictors. We are looking for a horizontal line with equally (random) spread points, such as the left. The right has room for improvement as they 'spread out' to the top right.

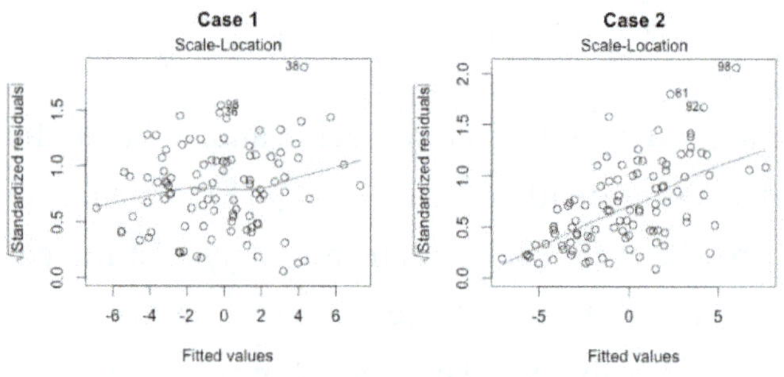

To summarize, residuals describe the data and linear model. A linear model may not be the best way to understand the data if there are many additional patterns that were overlooked. So evaluation of residuals is a great way to validate and gain insight into the underlying data.

While linear regression is widely used, other forms exist. These are often used when non-linear relationships exist or additional methods are needed to improve a model. Other regression techniques include polynomial regression, stepwise regression, ridge regression, lasso regression, and elasticnet regression.

CLASSIFICATION ALGORITHMS

Classification algorithms are a category of supervised algorithms that attempt to predict a categorical value, rather than numeric. This could be a simple dichotomous prediction of 'Yes' or 'No' or could include tens or hundreds of other categories, such as defect code, part type, customer demographics, etc. The input columns to a classification algorithm can be either numeric or categoric.

Classification algorithms can be segregated into parametric and non-parametric algorithms.

Parametric algorithms are those that summarize data with a set of fixed size parameters. Essentially, the amount of data used will not alter how many parameters needed. Example parametric algorithms are logistic regression, linear discriminate analysis, and Naïve Bayes. The benefits of parametric models are that they are quite simple and easier to understand and explain, they also perform rather quickly, and they do not require as much training data. Limitations of parametric algorithms are that they are not suitable for complex datasets and problems.

Non-parametric methods are useful with a large amount of data, no prior knowledge, and when a selection of the exact features is not suitable or possible. Non-parametric methods seek to find the best fit using training data while maintaining an ability to generalize on unseen data. Some examples of non-parametric models include k-Nearest Neighbor, Decision Trees, and Support Vector Machines. The benefits of non-parametric algorithms include the flexibility, the ability to make no assumptions about the underlying approach. The limitations include needing more data, being slower to train, and often overfit.

K-NEAREST NEIGHBOR

K-Nearest Neighbor, also referred to as kNN, was first proposed in 1951. As mentioned previously, kNN is a non-parametric and instance-based supervised learning algorithm.

Being non-parametric, it makes no explicit assumptions about the functional form, avoiding the dangers of mismodeling the underlying distribution of the data. When we say a technique is non-parametric, it means that it does not make any assumptions on the underlying data distribution. In other words, the model structure is determined from the data. This is useful since the 'real world' does not obey the typical theoretical assumptions made (as in linear regression models, for example). Therefore, KNN could and probably should be one of the first choices for a classification study when there is little or no prior knowledge about the distribution data.

Instance-based learning means that the algorithm does not learn a model as does other supervised algorithms. Therefore, kNN is often referred to as a lazy learner. Rather, it chooses to memorize the training instances, which are subsequently used as 'knowledge' to use during the prediction phase.

The Pseudocode

X = Training Data
Y = Class Labels of X; and x = unknown sample
For i=1 to m do
        Compute distance d(X$_i$, x)
End for
Compute set I containing indicies for the k smallest distances d(X$_i$,x).
Return majority label for {Y$_i$ where i ∈ I}

Consider the following diagram (Saxena, 2016):

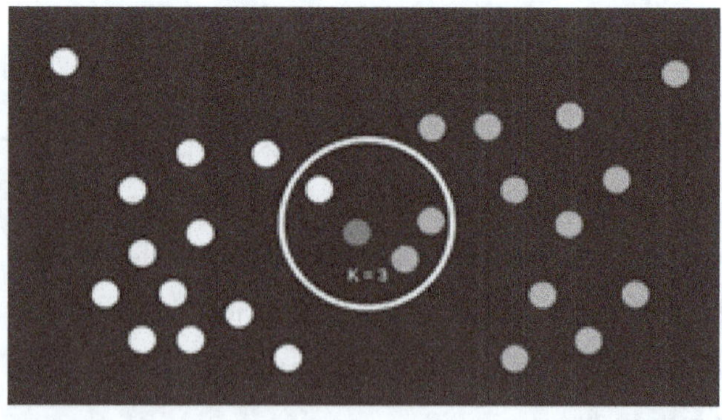

In this image, we have a total of 26 training observations across two classes, which are white and orange. With a new observation of blue, we would like to predict which class if falls within. With the k value as three, we next need to calculate the similarity distances using a similarity measure, such as Euclidean distance. The similarity score which is the lowest means it is closes to that class.

Choosing the proper k value is the most challenging aspect of the kNN algorithm. A smaller value means that noise will have a higher influence on the result – meaning, the likelihood of overfitting is high. A large value of k makes it computationally expensive. A rule of thumb is to start with the square root of n and adjust k based on the results.

The two common approaches to calculate distance is Euclidean and Manhattan.

Euclidean distance is the most common distance measure. The Euclidean distance between two points is the length of the path connecting them. The Pythagorean theorem provides the calculation between these two points.

Manhattan distance is the total sum of the difference between the x-coordinates and y-coordinates. To calculate this, the two points are measured along axes at right angles. As a general rule of thumb, Manhattan works better with a larger dimensional space.

The following diagram illustrates these two distances (Distances in Classification, 2016):

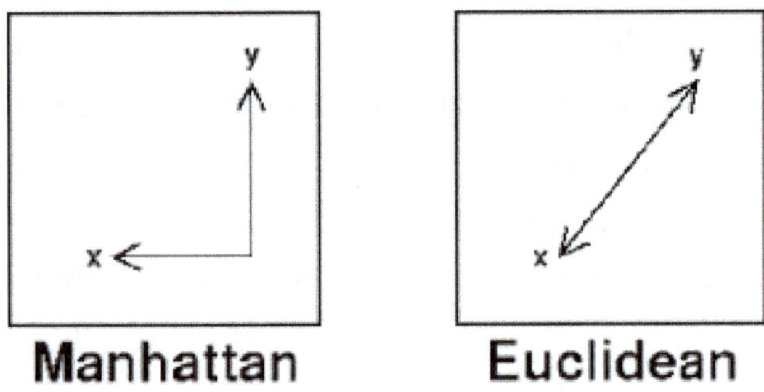

DECISION TREES

Decision trees are a very commonly used supervised classification algorithm that is also very easy to understand and communicate. Many variations to this exist, based on different approaches. A few of these include: ID3, C4.5, C5.0, CART, and CHAID. Although the details of each is slightly different, they are all based on the principle of greediness. Algorithms try to search for a variable which give the maximum information gain or divides the data in the most homogenous way.

The general goal of using Decision Tree is to train a model that can predict a class or value of the target variables by learning decision rules inferred from prior data (training data).

The Decision Tree Algorithm Pseudocode:

1.   Place the best attribute of the dataset at the root of the tree.

2.   Split the training set into subsets. Subsets should be made in such a way that each subset contains data with the same value for an attribute.

3.   Repeat step 1 and step 2 on each subset until you find leaf nodes in all the branches of the tree.

In decision trees, for predicting a class label for a record, we start from the root of the tree. First, the values of the root attribute are compared with the record's attribute. On the basis of comparison, we follow the branch corresponding to that value and jump to the next node. This comparison continues comparing the record's attribute values with other internal nodes of the tree until a leaf node is reached with predicted class value.

One of the primary challenges in creating decision trees is to identify which attributes we need to consider as the root node and each level. We have different attributes selection measure to identify the attribute which can be considered as the root note at each level. The two popular attribute selection measures are information gain, gain ratio, and gini index. These are used rather than random selection.

By using information gain as a criterion, we try to estimate the information contained by each attribute. We are going to use some points deducted from information theory. The randomness or uncertainty of a random variable X is defined by Entropy. Entropy is the measure of variability or randomness. Therefore, when using information gain, the decision tree will utilize the variable that gives us the maximum reduction in Entropy. Said another way, high variation attributes are often placed at the nodes/splits of the tree.

The challenge with information gain as a splitting mechanism is that it is biased towards multivalued attributes. To solve this, Gain Ratio emerged as an approach to overcome via taking into account the number of branches that would result before making the split. Therefore, gain ratio tends to prefer unbalanced splits where one partition is much smaller than another.

Gini index is the metric that measures how often a randomly chosen element would be incorrectly identified. It means an attribute with lower gini index should be used. Therefore, the split that gives us the maximum reduction in impurity is used for dividing the data. These splits favor equal-sized children.

To summarize:

Metrics	Drawback

Information Gain	Information Gain is biased towards multivariate attributes.
Gain Ratio	Gain Ratio generally prefers the unbalanced split of data where one of the child node has more number of entries compared to the others.
Gini Index	With more than 2 categories in the dataset, Gini Index gives unfavorable results. Apart from that it favors the split which results into equal sized children.

Decision tree algorithms often overfit on unseen data. Two common approaches are used to combat this outcome, which include pruning and early stopping.

Pruning is the simple approach to remove parts of the tree that do not provide help in classifying instances. To prune, cross-validation is used to train the model and the tree is pruned back until the cross-validated error is minimized.

An alternative approach to prevent overfitting is early stopping. Early stopping stops the tree-building process early, before it produces leaves with very small samples. To accomplish this, at each stage in splitting the tree, we can evaluate the cross-validation error. If the error does not decrease significantly enough, then we stop. If we prune too much, the tree may underfit on unseen data.

The various implementations of Decision Trees vary in their implementation approaches. The following provides a summary:

- ID3, or Iterative Dichotomizer, was the first decision tree implementation. The splitting criteria is based on Information Gain. The Attribute Types are only Categorical. No missing values are allowed.

- C4.5 & C5.0 – are improved versions of ID3, which accepts continuous values as well as categorical values. Missing values are allowed and splits using gain ratio. C5.0 improves upon C4.5 by allowing variable misclassification costs, since C4.5 treats all errors as equal.

- CART, or Classification and Regression Trees, uses the gini index approach to create binary splits. It can handle categorical or continuous values as well as missing values.

- CHAID, or Chi-squared Automatic Interaction Detector, uses a chi-squared based criterion instead of the information gain or gain ratio criteria to split. Chi-square is a test for independence that measures an association between two categorical variables. A statistically significant result indicates that the two variables are not independent. Chi-square tests are applied at each of the branch in building the tree, to ensure that each branch is associated with a statistically significant predictor of the response variable. Categorical and Continuous data may be used and handles missing values.

RANDOM FOREST AND BAGGING

The random forest algorithm emerged in 2001 by Leo Breiman and is an ensemble of decision trees. Ensembles can be thought of as a divide-and-conquer approach used to improve performance. This is accomplished via converting many 'weak learners' together to form a 'strong learner'. For instance, let us assume our goal is to predict fruit. If one tree can predict that the object is 3" in diameter, another that the object is round, and a third that the object is orange in color, then we can deduct that the object is an Orange. Neither of these three can do so alone, but when combined these 'weak learners' become quite strong and accurate at predicting this type of fruit.

The random forest algorithm randomly subsets samples from your dataset and builds a decision tree based on these samples. At each node in the tree mtry (a set parameter) number of features are selected from the set of all features. The best split feature using information gain is chosen and then the procedure is repeated. This algorithm is run on a large number of trees, typically starting at 500 and adjusted based on different sample subsets, which means that this method is less prone to overfitting than other tree methods.

Since each decision tree in the forest is only based on a subset of samples, from event the training dataset, each tree's performance can be evaluated on the left out samples. When this validation is performed on all samples and trees in a random forest, the resulting metric is called the out-of-bag (OOB) error. The advantage of using this metric is that it removes the need for a test set to evaluate the performance of your model.

The OOB can also be used to calculate variable importance across all the features in the model. Essentially, this illustrates the variables with the most predictive power. Variable importance is calculated by rerunning the random forest with one of the features values randomly scrambled across all samples. The difference in accuracy between the scrambled feature model and original model is the measure of variable importance. This is a very informative side-effect of this algorithm.

Random forests are not only useful for predictive models. They can also be very useful for feature selection (e.g., column identification for inclusion into a model) if a dataset has hundreds or thousands of input columns. Using random forest for this would need the identified variables to be validated on a test dataset.

The following steps cover the random forest process to building a model:

1) The algorithm first uses the Bagging (Bootstrap Aggregating) approach to create random samples. Given a data set S1 (n rows and p columns), it creates a new dataset (S2) by sampling n cases at random with replacement from the original data. About 1/3 of the rows from S1 are left out, known as Out of Bag(OOB) samples.

2) Then, the model trains on S2. OOB sample is used to determine unbiased estimate of the error.

3) Out of p columns, P << p columns are selected at each node in the data set. The P columns are selected at random. Usually, the default choice of P is sqrt(p) for classification trees.

4) Unlike a tree, no pruning takes place in random forest, meaning, each tree is grown fully.

5) Several trees are grown and the final prediction is obtained by averaging or voting.

Each tree is grown on a different sample of original data. Since random forest has the feature to calculate OOB error internally, cross validation is not really needed.

While bagging is used within random forest, it is not analogous to it. Bagging alone results in correlated trees when the underlying data has strong predictors. And, even averaging many highly correlated trees does not lead to a large reduction in variance. Said another way, we end up with many 'strong learners' from the strong predictors. So, we can derive that random forest extends bagging to use only a subset of features at the split (not all). This results in trees with different predictors at the top splits. This decorrelates the trees and achieves a more average output.

LOGISTIC REGRESSION

Logistic Regression is a type of regression that predicts the probability of occurrence of an event by fitting data to a logit function (logistic function). Like many forms of regression analysis, it makes use of several predictor variables that may be either numerical or categorical.

Logistic regression is the appropriate regression analysis to conduct when the dependent variable is dichotomous. Like all regression analyses, the logistic regression is a type of supervised predictive analysis. Logistic regression is used to describe data and to explain the relationship between one predictor binary variable and one or more nominal, ordinal, interval or ratio-level input variables.

Some of the assumptions of logistic regression include:

- The dependent variable should be dichotomous in nature (e.g., Yes or No).

- There should be no outliers in the data, which can be assessed by converting the continuous predictors to standardized scores, and removing values below -3.29 or greater than 3.29 (outlier definition at 3 standard deviations). This is called the 3-sigma rule.

- There should be no high correlations (multicollinearity) among the predictors. This can be assessed by a correlation matrix among the input variables and removing those that correlate above 0.90.

- At the center of the logistic regression analysis is the task estimating the log odds of an event.

Model fitting and the avoidance of overfitting should be considered when using logistic regressions. Adding independent variables to a logistic regression model will always increase the amount of variance explained in the log odds (typically expressed as R^2). However, adding more variables to the model can result in overfitting, which reduces the generalizability of the model beyond the data on which the model is fit.

Various pseudo-R2 values have been developed for logistic regression. These should be interpreted with extreme caution as they have many computational issues which cause them to be artificially high or low. A better approach is to present any of the goodness of fit tests available; Hosmer-Lemeshow is a commonly used measure of goodness of fit based on the Chi-square test. The Hosmer-Lemeshow test assesses whether or not the observed event rates match expected event rates in subgroups of the model population.

The central premise of Logistic Regression is the assumption that the input space can be separated into two nice 'regions', one for each class, by a linear (e.g., straight) line/boundary. A linear boundary for two dimensions is a straight line with no curving. For three dimensions, it is a plane. This boundary will be decided by the specific data. The data points must be separable into the two regions by a linear boundary. If your data points do satisfy this constraint, they are said to be linear-separable. Considering the example below (Joglekar, 2015).

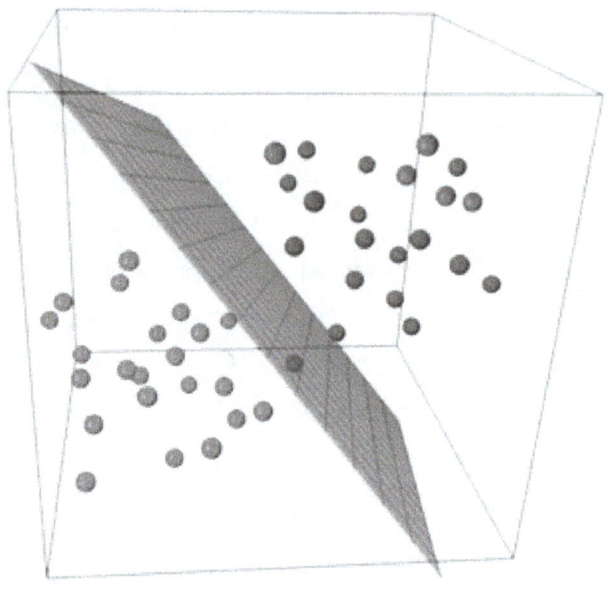

The green plane divides the two classes because it is linear in terms of its function as well as it helps discriminate between points belonging to different classes.

The output of a logistic regression model is much more informative than other classification algorithms. Like any regression approach, it expresses the relationship between an outcome / predictor variable (label) and each of its input features. The logistic regression not only gives a measure of how relevant a predictor is (coefficient size) but also its direction of association (positive or negative).

Comparing to a random forest, it will only tell you which predictors are more important to build the trees, without any information on the direction of association.

NAÏVE BAYES

The Naïve Bayes classification algorithm is based on Bayes' Theorem. This theorem makes the assumptions of independence of input features. Said another way, a Naïve Bayes classifier assumes that the presence of a particular feature in a class is unrelated to the presence of any other feature. For example, a fruit may be considered to be an apple if it is red, round, and about 3 inches in diameter. Even if these features depend on each other or upon the existence of the other features, all of these properties independently contribute to the probability that this fruit is an apple and that is why it is known as 'Naive'.

A Naive Bayes model is easy to build and particularly useful for very large data sets. Along with simplicity, Naive Bayes is known to outperform even highly sophisticated classification methods.

Bayes' Theorem is a way of calculating posterior probability. The algorithm is as follows:

$$P(c \mid x) = \frac{P(x \mid c)\,P(c)}{P(x)}$$

$$P(c \mid X) = P(x_1 \mid c) \times P(x_2 \mid c) \times \cdots \times P(x_n \mid c) \times P(c)$$

P(c|x) is the posterior probability of class (c, target) given predictor (x, attributes).

P(c) is the prior probability of class.

P(x|c) is the likelihood which is the probability of predictor given class.

P(x) is the prior probability of predictor.

Essentially, Naïve Bayes takes us from P(Evidence| Known Outcome) to P(Outcome|Known Evidence). We often know how frequently a scenario occurs,

138

given a known outcome. So, this is used to compute the reverse by computing the chance of that outcome occurring, given the evidence. This would occur via the following:

```
                              P(Likelihood of Evidence) * Prior prob of outcome
P(outcome|evidence) = _______________________________________________________
                                              P(Evidence)
```

The underlying goal is that by multiplying the prior, we give high probability to more common outcomes, and low probabilities to unlikely outcomes.

SUPPORT VECTOR MACHINES

Support Vector Machine (SVM) is another common Supervised Machine Learning algorithm that tries to maximize the gap between the categories of data.

A Maximum Margin Classifier is the simple way to divide your data if it is linearly separable. A Support Vector Classifier (SVC) is an extension to Maximum Margin Classifier where we allow some misclassification to occur. SVM is a further extension to SVC to accommodate non-linear boundaries. Although there is a clear distinction between various definitions, but people prefer to call all of them as SVM to avoid any complications. Logistic regression works well when we can create a linearly separate boundary, such as the image below (Support Vector Machines, 2018):

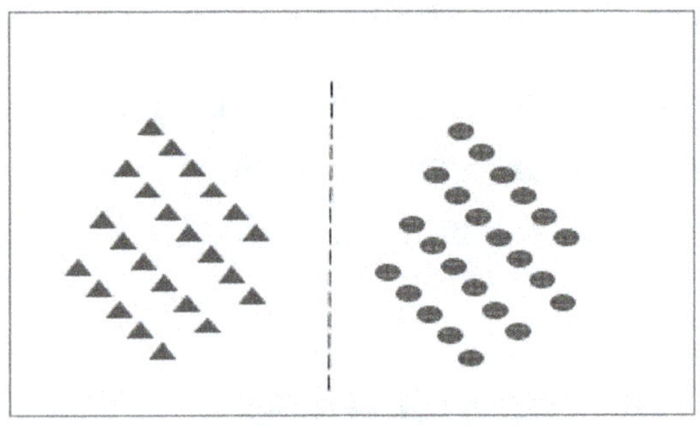

However, what if the blue triangle and red ovals are mixed, such as in the below image:

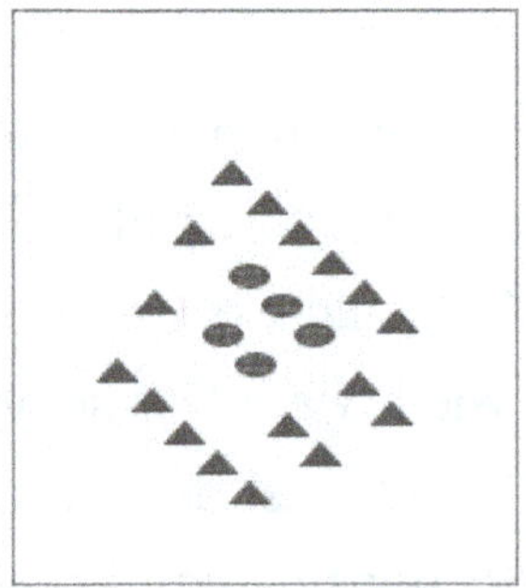

As we can see, in one-dimensional space (e.g., 1D), there is no clear line that can be derived. However, what would occur if we add additional dimensional spaces? In SVM, we use the term hyper-plane and the use of additional dimensions to create this boundary between classes, such as below:

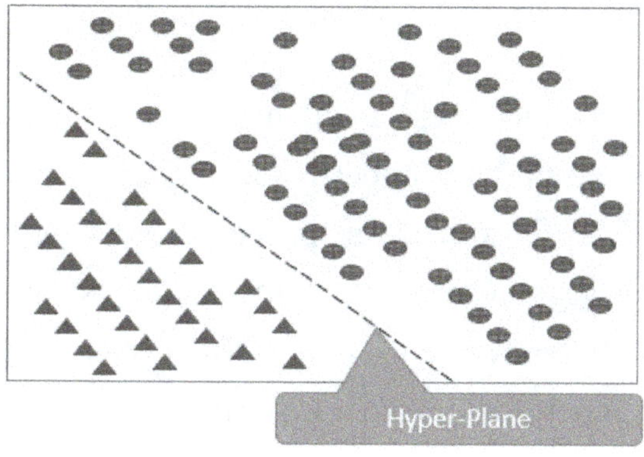

But, the challenge arises when we try to derive the hyperplane that creates the most divide between the classes. Consider the below image:

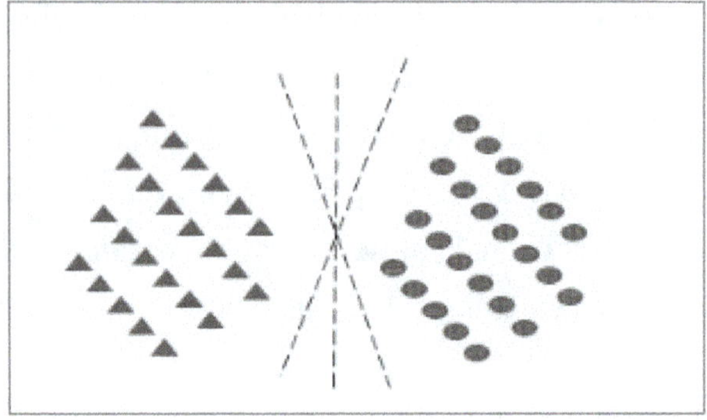

This diagram illustrates a dilemma for anyone trying to derive the best hyper-plane. This is where Maximum Margin Classifier provides assistance. Maximum Margin Classifier, helps to choose the optimal solution. The objective is to identify the separating hyperplane which is farthest from the observations. If we calculate the perpendicular distance from each point in training dataset to the separating hyperplanes, our optimal solution will have the plane with Maximum Margin. To simplify, if we insert a 'slab' to separate our data, the optimal solution will have the maximum width and the center line of the slab is called the hyperplane. See the slab image below:

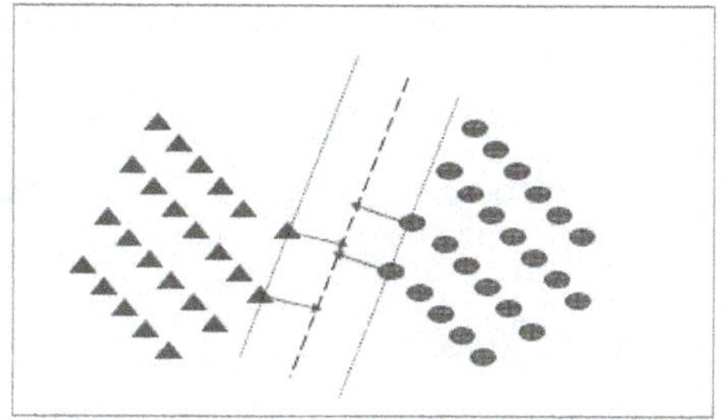

In the example shown above we can see that there are 4 points which are nearest to the boundary or are defining boundary, these points are called 'Support Vectors', hence the term Support Vector Machines.

The primary benefit of SVMs comes from the fact that they are not restricted to being linear classifiers. Although a bit more complex, by utilizing a technique known as the kernel trick, they can become much more flexible by introducing various types of non-linear decision boundaries.

The advantages of SVM include:

- The SVM is an effective tool in high-dimensional spaces, which is particularly applicable to document classification and sentiment analysis where the dimensionality can be very large.

- Since only a subset of the training points are used in the actual decision process of assigning new members, only these points need to be stored in memory (and calculated upon) when making decisions.

- Class separation is often highly non-linear. The ability to apply new kernels allows substantial flexibility for the decision boundaries, leading to greater classification performance.

Disadvantages

- In situations where the number of features for each object (p) exceeds the number of training data samples (n), SVMs can perform poorly. This can be seen intuitively, as if the high-dimensional feature space is much larger than the samples, then there are less effective support vectors on which to support the optimal linear hyperplanes, leading to poorer classification performance as new unseen samples are added.

- Since the classifier works by placing objects above and below a classifying hyperplane, there is no direct probabilistic interpretation for group membership. However, one potential metric to determine "effectiveness" of the classification is to assess the distance from the point to the decision boundary.

ADABOOST

Adaptive Boosting (Adaboost) is a technique that attempts to convert a weak learner into a strong learner. Considering the previous example of a fruit red, round, and about 3 inches in diameter, with each of these being a separate classifier, alone they are considered weak. Adaboost, similar to random forest, combines them in such a way that they become strong when used together.

Adaboost identifies weak rules via a base algorithm with a different distribution. Each time a base learning algorithm is applied, it generates a new weak prediction rule. After many iterations, the boosting algorithm combines these weak rules into a single strong prediction rule.

The following steps are used to choose a different distribution for each iteration:

1) The base learner takes all the distributions and assign equal weight or attention to each observation.

2) If there is any prediction error caused by first base learning algorithm, then we pay higher attention to observations having prediction error. Then, we apply the next base learning algorithm.

3) Iterate Step 2 till the limit of base learning algorithm is reached or higher accuracy is achieved.

4) The algorithm combines the outputs from weak learner and creates a strong learner which eventually improves the prediction power of the model. Boosting pays higher focus on examples which are mis-classified or have higher errors by preceding weak rules.

To see a visual example, consider the below image (Ray, 2015):

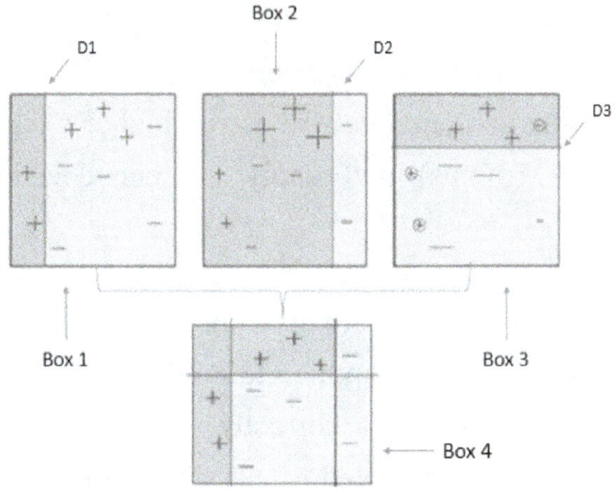

In Box 1, we have assigned equal weights to each data point and applied a decision stump to classify them as + (plus) or − (minus). The decision stump (D1) has generated vertical line at left side to classify the data points. This vertical line has incorrectly predicted three + (plus) as − (minus). In such case, we assign higher weights to these three + (plus) and apply another decision stump.

In Box 2, the size of three incorrectly predicted + (plus) is bigger as compared to rest of the data points. In this case, the second decision stump (D2) will try to predict them correctly. Now, a vertical line (D2) at right side of this box has classified three mis-classified + (plus) correctly. But again, it has caused mis-classification errors. This time with three -(minus). Again, we will assign higher weight to three – (minus) and apply another decision stump.

In Box 3, the – (minus) are given higher weights. A decision stump (D3) is applied to predict these mis-classified observations correctly. This time a horizontal line is generated to classify + (plus) and – (minus) based on higher weight of mis-classified observation.

In Box 4, D1, D2 and D3 have been combined to form a strong prediction having complex rule as compared to individual weak learner. You can see that this algorithm has classified these observations quite well as compared to any of individual weak learner.

So to summarize, AdaBoost first fits a 'sequence' of weak learners on different weighted training data. So boosting is created by sequentially adding weak learners versus ensembling and voting/averaging as in bagging. Boosting starts by predicting original data set and gives equal weight to each observation. If prediction is incorrect using the first learner, then it gives higher weight to observation which have been predicted incorrectly. Being an iterative process, it continues to add learner(s) until a limit is reached in the number of models or accuracy.

ARTIFICIAL NEURAL NETWORKS

Artificial Neural Networks (ANN) are an exciting and relatively new area of Machine Learning, and often referred to as Artificial Intelligence. ANN algorithms span both unsupervised and supervised learning. Some popular examples include speech-to-text, autonomous vehicle navigation, and language translation. The following diagram illustrates the architecture of various ANNs (Van Veen, 2016).

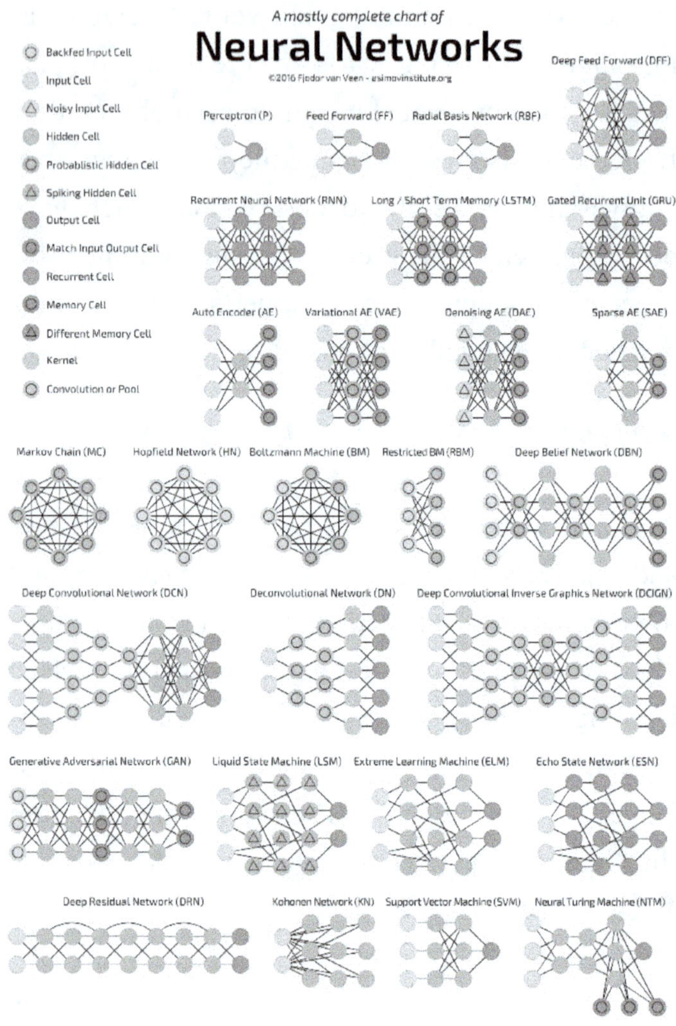

A mostly complete chart of
Neural Networks
©2016 Fjodor van Veen - asimovinstitute.org
Backfed Input Cell
Input Cell
Noisy Input Cell
Hidden Cell
Probablistic Hidden Cell
Spiking Hidden Cell
Output Cell
Match Input Output Cell
Recurrent Cell
Memory Cell
Different Memory Cell
Kernel
Convolution or Pool
Perceptron (P)
Feed Forward (FF)
Radial Basis Network (RBF)
Deep Feed Forward (DFF)
Recurrent Neural Network (RNN)
Long / Short Term Memory (LSTM)
Gated Recurrent Unit (GRU)
Auto Encoder (AE)
Variational AE (VAE)
Denoising AE (DAE)
Sparse AE (SAE)
Markov Chain (MC)
Hopfield Network (HN)
Boltzmann Machine (BM)
Restricted BM (RBM)
Deep Belief Network (DBN)
Deep Convolutional Network (DCN)
Deconvolutional Network (DN)
Deep Convolutional Inverse Graphics Network (DCIGN)
Generative Adversarial Network (GAN)
Liquid State Machine (LSM)
Extreme Learning Machine (ELM)
Echo State Network (ESN)
Deep Residual Network (DRN)
Kohonen Network (KN)
Support Vector Machine (SVM)
Neural Turing Machine (NTM)

Neural Networks are inspired by the biological neural networks of the human brain. Consider the following illustration of a neuron (Richard, 2018):

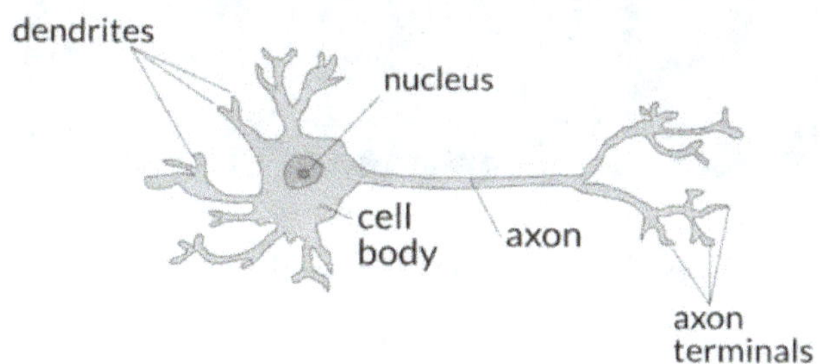

Considering this neuron, dendrites receive signals from other neurons and the cell body sums up all the incoming signals to generate input. When this sum reaches a threshold, the neuron fires down the axon to other neurons. This is called activation. Synapses are the point of connection from one neuron to another.

Our biological neural networks are arranged in a hierarchical manner so that certain neurons detect non-specific features in a more abstract way. For example, consider the fusiform face area of the brain, which is used for facial detection. The following image exercises this area of our brain as we determine if this image is a face (Shaikh, 2017):

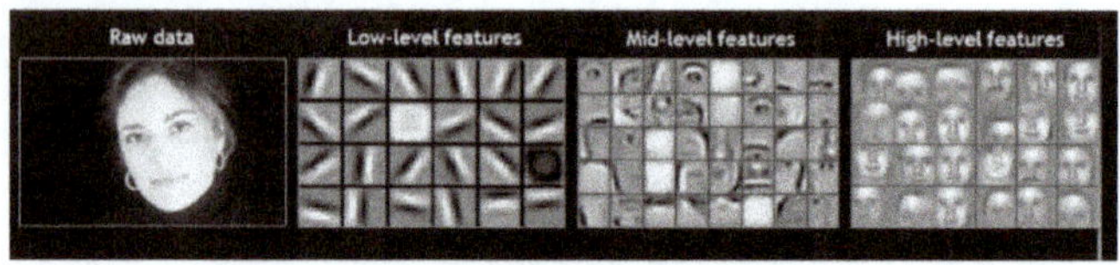

To compare the biological neural network to an artificial representation, consider the following image (Artificial Neural Networks, 2017):

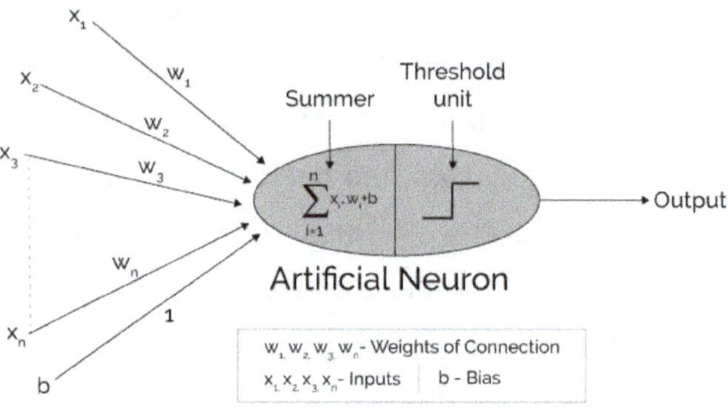

Considering this representation, X is the information from the external world (e.g., data input) and W is the input multiplied by the corresponding weights. The weights often represent the strength of connectivity between neurons and the training approach. The summer collects all the weighted inputs. And, the threshold establishes the activation method to get the desired output.

EVALUATION OF SUPERVISED ALGORITHMS

In practical terms, classification helps to uncover hidden relationships in your data. As discussed previously, many algorithm evaluation techniques exist to determine which to utilize. After all, the decision of which algorithm to finally deploy must be based on evaluation criteria, such as: ROC AUC, accuracy, precision and recall.

The 'No Free Lunch Theorem' states that no one algorithm works best in all scenarios. Meaning, it would be incorrect to state that "Random Forests are always the best algorithm". This is due to many characteristics of the desired goal, data quality, data distributions, and so on. Therefore, multiple algorithms should be assessed to determine which one is suitable for the data science project and goal.

TIME SERIES

Time-Series algorithms are widely used in econometrics. Time-series analysis involves utilization of sequences of data in chronological order, typically at regular and consistent intervals. This analysis can be applied to any variable that changes over time.

Five components consist within time-series analysis, which include level, noise, seasonality, trend, and cycle. The level is simply the mean of a series of events under evaluation. The noise is often referred to as the randomness of the data and these are observations that are not correlated with any explained trends. Seasonality occurs if the data has regular and predictable fluctuations in the series that are correlated with the calendar. Trend refers to the data having a long-term projection that shifts to a positive or negative direction. Finally, cycle refers to repeating periods that are not related to the calendar.

HOLT-WINTERS (TRIPLE EXPONENTIAL SMOOTHING)

Holt-Winters, also referred to as Triple Exponential Smoothing, assigns exponentially decreasing weights for newest to oldest observations. In other words, the older the data, the less priority ('weight') the data is given; newer data is seen as more relevant and is assigned more weight. Smoothing parameters, usually denoted by α, determine the weights for observations.

Exponential smoothing is usually used to make short term forecasts, as longer-term forecasts using this technique can be quite unreliable.

Some characteristics of Holt-Winters include:

- Simple (single) exponential smoothing uses a weighted moving average with exponentially decreasing weights.

- Holt's trend-corrected double exponential smoothing is usually more reliable for handling data that shows trends, compared to the single procedure.

- Triple exponential smoothing (also called the Multiplicative Holt-Winters) is usually more reliable for parabolic trends or data that shows trends and seasonality.

If the data under evaluation illustrates trend and seasonality, then Holt-Winters may be useful.

ARIMA

Autoregressive Integrated Move Average Models (ARIMA) is a forecasting technique that projects the future values of a series based entirely on its own inertia. ARIMA is primarily used in short-term forecasting requiring at least 40 historical data points. ARIMA works best when your data include stable or consistent patterns over time with a minimum amount of outliers. ARIMA is usually superior to exponential smoothing techniques when the data is reasonably long and the correlation between past observations is stable. If the data is short or highly volatile, then some other smoothing method may perform better. If you do not have at least 40 data points, you should consider some other method than ARIMA.

The first step in applying ARIMA methodology is to check for stationarity. Stationarity evaluates the series to ensure it remains at a fairly constant level over time. If a trend exists, as in most economic or business applications, then the data is not stationary. The data should also show a constant variance in its fluctuations over time. This is easily seen with a series that is heavily seasonal and growing at a faster rate. In such a case, the peaks and valleys in the seasonality will become more dramatic over time. Without these stationarity conditions being met, many of the calculations associated with the process cannot be computed.

If a graphical plot of the data indicates non-stationarity, then differencing should be applied to the series. Differencing is a technique of transforming a non-stationary series to a stationary series. This is accomplished by subtracting the observation in the current period from the previous one. If this transformation is done only once to a series, you say that the data has been 'first differenced'. This process essentially eliminates the trend if your series is growing at a fairly constant rate. If it is growing at an increasing rate, you can apply the same procedure and difference the data again. Your data would then be 'second differenced', etc.

In ARIMA, 'autocorrelations' are numerical values that indicate how a data series relates to itself over time. More precisely, it measures how strongly the data values at a specified number of periods apart are correlated to each other over time. The number of periods apart is usually called the 'lag'. For example, an autocorrelation at lag 1 measures how values 1 period apart are correlated to one another throughout the series. An autocorrelation at lag 2 measures how the data two periods apart are correlated throughout the series. Autocorrelations may range from +1 to -1. A value close to +1 indicates a high positive correlation while a value close to -1 implies a high negative correlation. These measures are most often evaluated through graphical plots called "correlagrams". A correlagram plots the auto- correlation values for a given series at different lags. This is referred to as the 'autocorrelation function' and is very important in the ARIMA method.

The ARIMA approach attempts to describe the movements in a stationary time series as a function of what are called "autoregressive and moving average" parameters. These are referred to as AR parameters (auto-regressive) and MA parameters (moving averages).

The pseudocode for ARIMA with one parameter is:

$$X(t) = A(1) * X(t-1) + E(t)$$

where X(t) = time series under investigation

A(1) = the autoregressive parameter of order 1

X(t-1) = the time series lagged 1 period

E(t) = the error term of the model

This simply means that any given value X(t) can be explained by some function of its previous value that occurred, X(t-1), plus some unexplainable random error, E(t). If the estimated value of A(1) was .40, then the current value of the series would be related to 40% of its value 1 period ago. Of course, the series could be related to more than just one past value.

For example,

$$X(t) = A(1) * X(t-1) + A(2) * X(t-2) + E(t)$$

This indicates that the current value of the series is a combination of the two immediately preceding values, X(t-1) and X(t-2), plus some random error E(t). Our model is now an autoregressive model of order 2.

CONCLUSION

Data Science has been referred to as the 'Sexiest Job of the 21st Century'. Given we generate massive amounts of data as we go about our daily lives, this data exhibits many trends that can improve our qualities of life. This data exhaust can now be used for many scenarios, such as:

- Improved marketing, such as market-basket analysis to recommend associated products we may not realize is available or needed.

- With chatbots such as Alexa, Siri, Cortana, and others, we can now simply ask our device to order a product.

- Smart-home devices are rapidly increasing. Now, home automation can span thermostats, door-locks, light switches, microwaves, timers, power adapters for lamps, and many other growing areas. Using simple machine learning recommendations such as a thermostat, patterns in settings can be derived and recommended or used in an autonomous way.

- Autonomous vehicles are now pervasive in many industries. This could be a part delivery cart on a manufacturing floor, unmanned aircraft, lane-keep assist on a modern automobile, or complete autonomy of an automobile. With the ability to identify and detect objects using advanced neural net algorithms, we can deduct that this will continue to expand.

- Chatbots can now be used to assist with mining massive amounts of data and guide users in scenarios such as helpdesk calls, human resource questions, and general knowledge mining. For instance, any modern smartphone provides the capability ask 'What is the weather tomorrow' or 'Which team won the football game'.

- Robotic Process Automation is a growing area of business operations. These tools essentially create simple to complex macros to automate mundane tasks. An example may be a repetitive task that includes opening an email, opening an attachment, reading the values, and keying them into the Enterprise Resource Planning (ERP) System. Via defining this macro, employees can be moved to more gratifying and useful tasks.

While this is only a short list of scenarios, we can deduct that these will continue to expand. Many software and IT suppliers are currently expanding their products to partner with Machine Learning tools provides or include inherently within their products. The future is bright and ever evolving in the area of Data Science!

References

Desjardins, J (2017). How Many Millions of Lines of Code Does it Take? Retrieved from: http://www.visualcapitalist.com/millions-lines-of-code/

Randell, B. (1968). The 1968/69 NATO Software Engineering Report. Retrieved from http://homepages.cs.ncl.ac.uk/brian.randell/NATO/NATOReports/

Lewis, L. (2018). 2018 Update: What Happens in an Internet Minute. Retrieved from https://www.allaccess.com/merge/archive/28030/2018-update-what-happens-in-an-internet-minute#sthash.IKyiTou1.uxfs

McCarthy, J., Minsky, M., Rochester, N., Shannon, C.E. (1955). A Proposal for the Dartmouth Summer Research Project on Artificial Intelligence. Retrieved from http://raysolomonoff.com/dartmouth/boxa/dart564props.pdf

O'Neil, C. & Schutt, Rachel, S. (2013). Doing Data Science. O'Reilly Media, Inc. ISBN: 9781449363871. Retrieved from https://www.safaribooksonline.com/library/view/doing-data-science/9781449363871/

Piatetsky, G. (2018). Surprises in Analytics, Data Science, Machine Learning Software Poll. Retrieved from https://www.kdnuggets.com/2017/05/poll-analytics-data-science-machine-learning-software-leaders.html

Edwards, C. (2018). Deep Learning Hunts for Signals Among the Noise. ACM 61(6). 10.1145/3204445 Retrieved from https://cacm.acm.org/magazines/2018/6/228030-deep-learning-hunts-for-signals-among-the-noise/fulltext

Taylor, J. (2017). Four Problems in Using CRISP-DM and How to Fix Them. Retrieved from https://www.kdnuggets.com/2017/01/four-problems-crisp-dm-fix.html

Soni, D. (2018). Supervised vs. Unsupervised Learning. Retrieved from https://towardsdatascience.com/supervised-vs-unsupervised-learning-14f68e32ea8d

Cathy, M. (2018). Correlation versus Causation. Retrieved from https://teacher.desmos.com/activitybuilder/custom/58a2545837a69a9207b5fe99#preview/f637d8c2-11a5-4e31-a224-98ebb348ccaf

Seif, G. (2018). 5 Quick and Easy Data Visualizations in Python with Code. Retrieved from https://towardsdatascience.com/5-quick-and-easy-data-visualizations-in-python-with-code-a2284bae952f

Belludi, N. (2008). Albertg Mehrabian's 7-38-55 Rule of Personal Communication. Retrieved from http://www.rightattitudes.com/2008/10/04/7-38-55-rule-personal-communication/

Dykes, B. (2016). Data Storytelling: The Essential Data Science Skill Everyone Needs. Retrieved from https://www.forbes.com/sites/brentdykes/2016/03/31/data-storytelling-the-essential-data-science-skill-everyone-needs/#43b0529052ad

Damosio, A. (2009). When Emotions Make Better Decisions – Antonio Damasio. Retrieved from https://www.youtube.com/watch?v=1wup_K2WN0I

Rosenberg, E. (2014). 1854 Broad Street cholera outbreak map. Retrieved from https://sites.google.com/a/rmscollab.net/roosevelt-science/word-of-the-week/1854broadstreetcholeraoutbreakmap?overridemobile=true

Peterson, L. (2018). Unsupervised Learning. Retrieved from https://medium.com/vody-

techblog/unsupervised-learning-
a6438958f1b8

Markman, K. (2015). Comparing supervised
learning algorithms. Retrieved from
http://www.dataschool.io/comparing-
supervised-learning-algorithms/

Forster, A. (2014). Machine Learning for Body
Sensor Networks. Retrieved from
http://www.slideshare.net/annafoerster/mach
ine-learning-for-body-sensor-networks

(2018). What is a Dendrogram? Retrieved from
https://www.displayr.com/what-is-
dendrogram/

Veress, G. (2013). Cluster Training. Retrieved
from
https://www.slideshare.net/gveress/cluster-
training-2013

Raschka, S. (2014). Linear Discriminate Analysis.
Retrieved from
https://sebastianraschka.com/Articles/2014_
python_lda.html

Sayad, S. (2019). Association Rules. Retrieved from
https://www.saedsayad.com/association_rule
s.htm

Kelley, R. (2017). Making Predictive Models
Robust: Holdout vs Cross-Validation.
Retrieved from
https://www.kdnuggets.com/2017/08/dataik
u-predictive-model-holdout-cross-
validation.html

Raschka, S. (2018). Linear Regression via Least
Squares Fit Method. Retrieved from
https://relate.cs.illinois.edu/course/cs357-
f15/file-
version/68fa8dd5f1a58eb5d5e81218d37a59f
892ca861b/media/least-
squares/linregr_least_squares_fit.html

Bommae, K. (2015). Understanding Diagnostic
Plots for Linear Regression Analysis.
Retrieved from
https://data.library.virginia.edu/diagnostic-
plots/

Saxena, R. (2016). KNN Classifier, Introduction to K-Nearest Neighbor Algorithm. Retrieved from http://dataaspirant.com/2016/12/23/k-nearest-neighbor-classifier-intro/

(2016). Distances in Classification. Retrieved from http://www.ieee.ma/uaesb/pdf/distances-in-classification.pdf

Joglekar, S. (2015). Logistic Regression. Retrieved from https://codesachin.wordpress.com/2015/08/16/logistic-regression-for-dummies/

(2018). Support Vector Machine (SVM). Retrieved from https://www.dezyre.com/data-science-in-r-programming-tutorial/support-vector-machine-tutorial

Spruyt, V. (2018) What are eigenvectors and eigenvalues? Retrieved from http://www.visiondummy.com/2014/03/eigenvalues-eigenvectors/

Ray, S. (2015). Quick Introduction to Boosting Algorithms in Machine Learning. Retrieved

from
https://www.analyticsvidhya.com/blog/2015
/11/quick-introduction-boosting-algorithms-
machine-learning/

Van Veen, F. (2016). The Neural Network Zoo.
Retrieved from
http://www.asimovinstitute.org/neural-
network-zoo/

Shaikh, F. (2017). Deep Learning vs. Machine
Learning – the essential differences you
need to know! Retrieved from
https://www.analyticsvidhya.com/blog/2017
/04/comparison-between-deep-learning-
machine-learning/

Richard, N. (2018). The differences between
Artificial and Biological Neural Networks.
Retrieved from
https://towardsdatascience.com/the-
differences-between-artificial-and-
biological-neural-networks-a8b46db828b7

(2017). Artificial Neural Networks, Neural
Networks Applications and Algorithms.

Retrieved from
https://www.xenonstack.com/blog/data-science/artificial-neural-networks-applications-algorithms/